£39-50

A9m

D1203798

Architectural Press Library of Planning and Design

Fitting out the Workplace

Fitting out the Workplace

John Worthington and Allan Konya

A straightforward guide for the layman and professional to the specification of workplace interiors

The Architectural Press: London

First published in 1988 by
the Architectural Press, 9 Queen
Anne's Gate, London SW1H 9BY

**British Library Cataloguing in
Publication Data**
Worthington, John
  Fitting out the workplace
  1. Interior decoration
  2. Work environment
  I. Title II. Konya, Allan
  747'85 NK2113
ISBN 0-85139-995-9

Typeset by Crawley Composition Ltd
Printed in Great Britain at the University Press, Cambridge

Contents

Acknowledgments

Small dynamic firms have diverse demands in the types of activity and the levels of specification they wish to provide in their place of work. The concept for this book originated from a tenants' fit-out manual prepared by DEGW for Warrington and Runcorn Development Corporation's multi-tenanted Genesis Business Centre at Birchwood Science Park. The advice here encapsulates DEGW's experience of working for a wide variety of both small and large organisations.

Special thanks to Paul Stansall, who prepared the case study material, to Sue Dawson for editorial assistance, to Martin Shirley for the shell and fit-out diagrams, to John Desmond of Bernard Williams Associates for cost information, and to Annette Gardner for tireless typing and corrections.

Lastly, the project would not have reached fruition without the exactitude and clear thinking of Allan Konya, who completed Part III and the Appendices.

John Worthington

PART 1

The Context

Introduction

The need for a book such as this 25 years ago would have found little recognition. Organisations at that time fell into two categories: those which were small and craft orientated and had simple requirements; and large, well established organisations that would plan and design a factory or office environment for themselves with the help of consultants. The number of building components that could be bought from catalogues was limited. The norm was to design each factory or office interior individually, each fit out invariably being considered as an integral part of the building design. Within this framework the architect would offer his traditional services of design, specification and supervision according to the RIBA plan of work.

The intervening years have seen a major shift in focus. Today there is a wide selection of products that can be bought off the peg to help a tenant adapt a building to his individual requirements. There are a variety of ways to get building work done. Small firms are now more sophisticated in the range of their activities and equipment they use and in the quality of the environment that they require. Moreover, custom designed buildings have given way to ready-to-use building shells which can be fitted out with off-the-peg components to meet specific tenant needs. Architects may expect to find themselves competing with 'design and build' services, and product suppliers who provide an advice and installation service. If architects wish to continue to work in this field they may need to adapt their skills and services to compete.

This manual deals with the needs of the firm of 50 or less staff with below 15,000 ft^2 of space who have space or a building which they wish to adapt to their individual pattern of work. The book is not concerned with how to maintain or adapt the fabric, but rather with the elements that can be added to the building shell to change the character, quality and environment.

The Tenant's Dilemma

Finding and procuring space is only half the problem a firm faces when considering new premises. Once space is found it must be adapted to meet specific requirements. Individual offices may have to be built, floor finishes changed or even mechanical extract and additional power installed for a complex piece of equipment. The quality of finishes,

ceilings and lighting may also need to be improved in the visitors' reception area. All these are items which will have to be added to the basic space as leasehold improvements.

The objective of *Fitting out the Workplace* is to provide:

— Guidance to owners or managers of small businesses and their architects and advisers on the components available to adjust finishes, change the capacity of servicing, provide subdivision, control and adapt the climatic

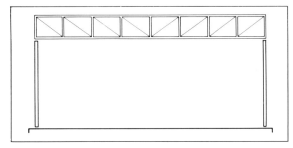
(a)

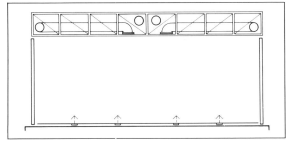
(b)

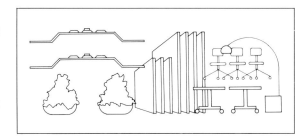
(c)

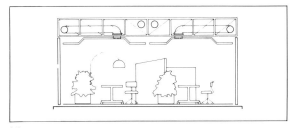
(d)

Figure 1. Building design decisions reflect different timescales:
a) Building shells have a life span of 75 years and may have many owners.
b) Services have a life span of 15 years and adjust one shell to specific functions.
c) Scenery may change every 5-7 years as organisations grown and change.
d) On a daily, weekly or monthly basis, scenery may be moved to reflect specific activities.

environment and make the most effective use of space.

— An index of components available on the market for different functions, classified according to cost and level of sophistication.

— A simple explanation of the fitting-out process and procurement options.

— Pertinent case-study material, to help small firms plan their own work and show opportunities.

Shell, Scenery and Settings

Buildings take a long time to build, are difficult to change, and once built are there to last. Firms, on the other hand, are continuously in a state of flux, as the economy, technology and market changes around them. To reduce the problem of organisations becoming straightjacketed by their buildings, it is possible to conceive a premises strategy with several layers of decision, each with its own time scale, **1**.

First, we have the container, or *building shell*, within which the activities are housed. The shell has a time scale of at least 75 years, reflecting the permanence of the materials it is made of and real estate values. The shell may see several changes of occupant and many changes of activity through its lifespan. The environment within the shell and the range of activities it can accommodate is a result of the services installed. *Services* have a life expectancy of probably 15 years, and possibly even less as the pace of technological change increases.

The shell is adapted to a specific firm's requirements by *scenery*: finishes, ceilings, lighting fixtures, furniture, etc. Scenery, which typically has a life expectancy of 5–7 years, depending on its specification, reflects the style and function of the organisation. Scenery can, on a day-to-day basis, be rearranged to form different *settings* to reflect short-term needs of the organisation.

This book is concerned with the choice of scenery elements, and freestanding service components independent of the structure of the building. It is a guide to help with short-term adjustments, not a manual to major fitting-out projects.

Changing Demands on the Workplace

Employment opportunities are shifting from manufacturing to service and office functions. The move is from large scale manufacturing processes, consisting of firms with long production runs, to small scale, consisting of short production runs, with a mixture of office, laboratory, distribution and assembly functions in the same building, **2**. The reason is easy to

Figure 2. Manufacturing firms are moving to short runs and often a mix of functions in the same building.
a) Research.
b) Assembly.
c) Marketing.
d) Training.

(a)

(c)

(b)

(d)

*Figure 3.
Building shells
may be adapted
to a firm's
individual
requirements by
using complete
furniture
systems, such
as Herman Miller
Action Factory.*

see. The expanding sectors of the economy rely for their success on the application of very specialised and advancing knowledge and the harnessing of new technologies. As production processes become more mechanised the balance of human effort shifts towards management and invention and away from straightforward production.

A healthy firm must continuously adapt its product or service to the needs of customers and to the latest technology available. To provide a flexible response, the trend is for firms to become more integrated, with manufacturing research, design administration and sales (who act as the antennae to the marketplace) often in the same building. The increased speed of technological innovation not only means shorter productions runs and an integration of functions, but also the need to be able to rapidly change interior layouts and adapt to new processes. The result has been a shift from custom designed buildings with tailored interior layouts to loosely fitting, pre-designed, ready-to-use shells with a flexible set of interior components, **3**.

Part III of the book provides an easily accessible list of the components available to adjust both the old existing building stock and the new, speculative office or industrial space, for office, laboratory or industrial users.

Differing organisational requirements

The character of a firm's accommodation and the choice of components and materials for the interior reflect the organisation and its function. The main organisational variables and their fitting-out implications are listed below in left- and right-hand columns respectively:

Age of firm

Firms, like families, go through a life cycle, from embryonic beginnings and youth to established expectations, and the sophistication of specification will reflect the firm's maturity. (Table 1)
— Size of budget/quality of finishes.
— Degree of permanence required.
— Type of funding (leased or bought).

Table 1 The premises ladder: a firm's expectations and premises requirements change according to their stage in the life cycle.

	Type of building	Time span of decisions	Method of adaptation
MATURE Professional management	Independent building	Own building	Structural and services changes
		5-year plan	Full professional service and main contractor
YOUTHFUL A small group of employees with a basic management	Part of building with own front door	Long lease with review periods	Limited structural adaptation
		Year by year	Professional advice sub-contractors
INFANT Independent firm supporting a handful of staff	Several rooms in larger building	Short lease	Partitions new floor, finishes decoration, add-on services
			Professional advice, direct labour, component suppliers and installation team
EMBRYO	Desk within somebody else's space	Licence	As found – second-hand desks and chairs
		Month by month	Do-it-yourself

4

Table 2 The accommodation requirements of three different business activities in clothing, furniture and electronics, according to their motivation and style of development.

Type of firm	Embryonic	Infant
CLOTHING craft	Hand knitting, bespoke clothes with design input, screen printed fabrics, costumes Work at home, adult education classes, community workshop, craft workshop	Working community Independent small studio
Opportunistic	Short runs of garments, fashion garments, silk screening on sweat shirts, and distribution Spare room, garage, sub-leased space in established firm Outworkers	Garment batch production Distribution and coordination of outworkers Separate space in flatted factory Short life industrial building
FURNITURE craft	Individual designed pieces, cabinet work and repair Antique sales and repair Back yard, community workshop, new enterprise workshop, skill centre	Independent workshop Working community
Opportunistic	Batch production of simple pieces. Second-hand furniture Back yard Short life shop	Starter unit Shop front
ELECTRONICS craft	Production of prototypes or components Adult education classes, technical college, front room	Flatted factory Working community
Opportunistic	Assembly and distribution of parts Coordination of outworkers and mail order distribution Space in larger organisation Innovation centre	Warehouse Starter units Separate space in larger organisation

Expectations of firm

Firms may be typecast as *craft*, where the founder wishes to continue to do the work, and not expand; or *opportunistic*, where the ambition of the founder is to mechanise and rationalise the process, and expand. (Table 2)
— Quality and choice of finish.
— Degree of adaptability required.
— Amount of built-in, rather then freestanding, furniture and equipment.
— Level of servicing.

Size of firm

1–5 (workroom, studio, office suite)
5–15 (workshop, showroom, office)
15–50 (factory, office)
— Amount of fitting out required.
— Choice of procurement procedure and implementation.

Density of people/equipment

The density of occupancy reflects the amount of equipment or storage required, **4**.
— Number of services required.
— Amount of partitioning.
— Sophistication of specification.
— Lighting and heating levels.

Sophistication of production/process

Production process may be low or high technology, and individual batch or line production runs.
— Levels of services.
— Sophistication of environmental controls.
— Type of furniture and equipment.
— Type of spatial organisation of interior.

Size of working groups

Some firms may work as individuals, with small support groups (e.g. lawyers), whereas others work in project teams (design office).
— Amount of partitioning or screening required.
— Lighting and ceiling finish.

Figure 4.
The density of building use depends on the activities being undertaken.
a) Typical office use; one person per 8 m² of floor area.
b) Printing firm; one person per 30 m² of floor area.
c) Storage and distribution; one person per 60 m² of floor area.

Degree of privacy or security required by individual activities

— Amount and type of partitioning.

Deliveries and visitors

The frequency of visitor contact will be reflected in the degree of prestige required.
— Quality and finishes.
— External accessories.
The quality and character of fitting out may, as well as reflecting the style of the organisation, vary within the same tenancy to respond to the different functions being accommodated. Within a single firm's premises it is possible to have at least four qualities of specification (Table 3), each tailored to the needs of a specific activity.

The Types of Building Shells Available

For the majority of smaller firms the opportunity to move into a purpose designed building is rare. Most firms will be confronted with the choice, having found the most suitable location, of finding a vacant building or part of a building and adapting it to their own requirements. The buildings available for rent may be:
— New speculative units, **5a**.
— 'Second-hand' industrial or office stock built in the last 30 years and now available on the market, **5b**.
— Redundant premises, where the original use is no longer relevant, such as schools, warehouses, or hospitals, **5c**.
When assessing the buildings available and deciding which might be suitable for a particular firm's needs, the following characteristics should be borne in mind:

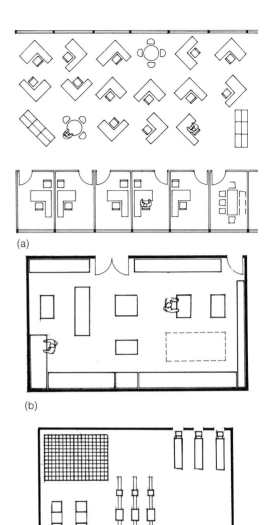

(a)

(b)

(c)

Table 3 Within the same building shell specifications may vary to reflect the needs of each activity.				
	Storage/ distribution	*Industrial*	*Office*	*Public areas*
Sub-division	Minimum 0–10% of floor area Basic finishes	10–20% of floor area Basic finishes, glazed fronts	20–60% of floor area	Quality finishes
Services		Air handling for localised machines	Air handling for localised machines and meeting areas	Air handling for meeting and presentation spaces
Floor	Hard surfaces	Carpet or hard surfaces	Carpet	Carpet
Ceiling	Exposed structure, suspended lighting	Exposed structure or suspended ceiling for assembly functions	Suspended or open ceiling Acoustic	Suspended ceiling, recessed lighting

Figure 5.
a) Advanced
   factory
   building shell.
b) Speculative
   1960s office
   stock.
c) Redundant
   pre-war
   industrial
   shell (next
   page).

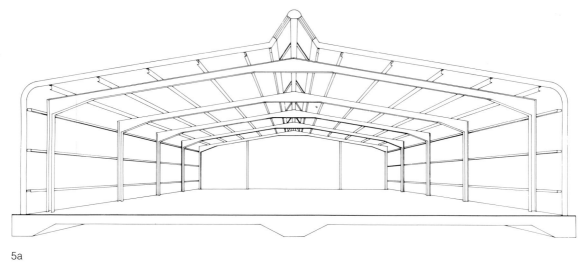

5a

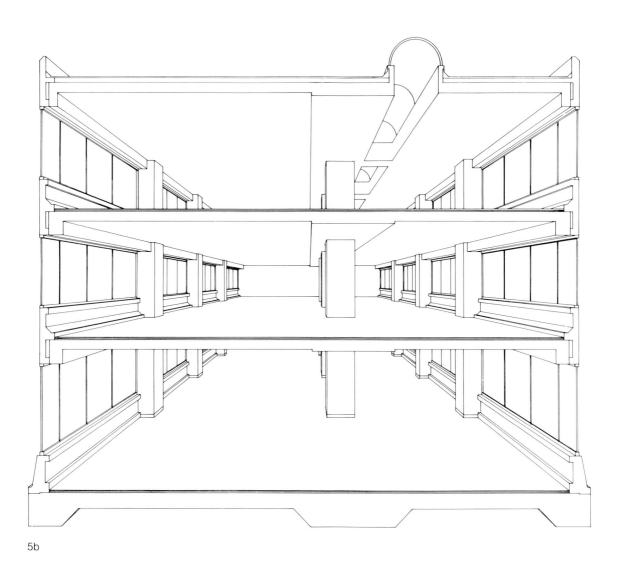

5b

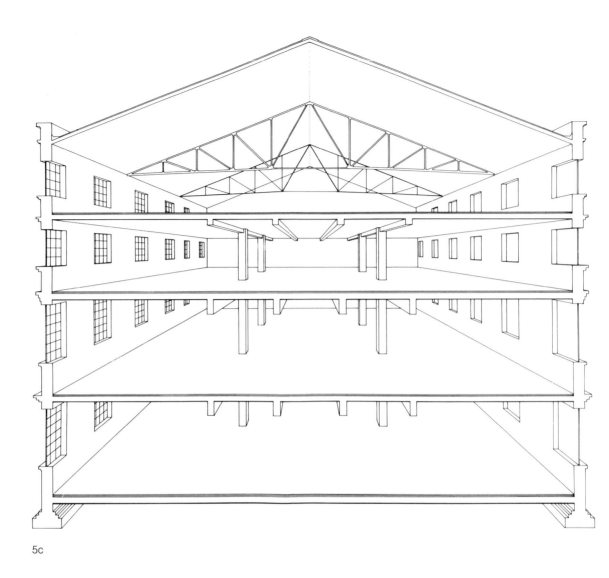

5c

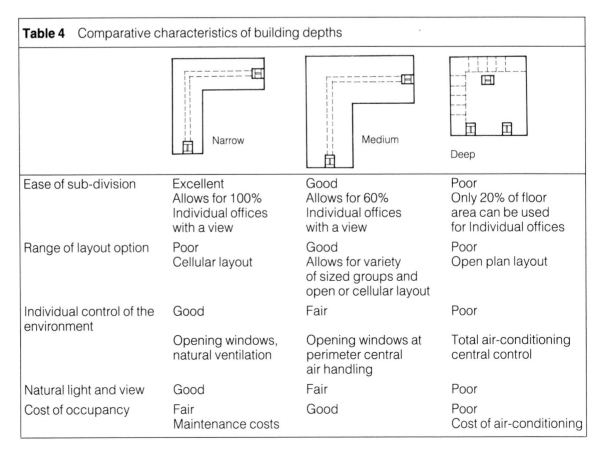

Table 4	Comparative characteristics of building depths		
	Narrow	Medium	Deep
Ease of sub-division	Excellent Allows for 100% Individual offices with a view	Good Allows for 60% Individual offices with a view	Poor Only 20% of floor area can be used for Individual offices
Range of layout option	Poor Cellular layout	Good Allows for variety of sized groups and open or cellular layout	Poor Open plan layout
Individual control of the environment	Good Opening windows, natural ventilation	Fair Opening windows at perimeter central air handling	Poor Total air-conditioning central control
Natural light and view	Good	Fair	Poor
Cost of occupancy	Fair Maintenance costs	Good	Poor Cost of air-conditioning

Size: match the firm's demands against the following questions:
- What is the overall size of the building?
- How much space is available on each floor?
- How much of the space is usable, compared with the amount of space required for circulations services and structure?

Building shape: the ease with which the firm's organisation will fit into the building will be influenced by the answers to questions such as:
- The shape of each floor?
- The number of different shaped floors?
- The distance between vertical circulation points?

Construction: planning flexibility and the ease of adaptation will be dependent on how easily walls can be moved and internal cladding changed.

Width of floors: the ability to provide enclosed offices with a view, provide natural light and ventilation or accommodate small working groups is related to the width across the building (Table 4). 12–15 m (40–50 ft) narrow depth buildings allow for a high percentage of cellular offices and small working groups. Deeper spaces 18 m (60 ft) or above will need mechanical ventilation and artificial lighting for high density uses.

Number of floors: affects the ease of delivery access, and internal communication within the organisation, depending on the size of each floor.

Floor to floor: the amount of clearance provided will influence the amount of servicing that can be accommodated, the ability to add an intermediate mezzanine floor or the installation of special equipment or goods handling systems.

Servicing: the shell may simply be a 'raw space' with water, power and waste pipes to the perimeter, or be fully fitted out with lighting, heating, ducting for mechanical ventilation and plumbing.

Condition: the size of the budget required for adapting and fitting out the shell depends on the condition of the building structure and fabric, its ability to meet current statutory requirements (fire, health, etc) and the quality of finishes and services. Table 5 summarises five categories of condition that may be expected and the commitment required with each.

New speculatively designed units

These may either be classified as industrial or office accommodation, with a new category recently appearing called Scientific or 'high tech' uses that provide for a mixture of office and light industrial uses, as in **5a**. Now formally encompassed by the 'Business Use Class'.

Industrial

New units will normally be found on industrial estates, and marketed as nursery units (below 2500 ft^2 units). Small manufacturing units (2500–15,000 ft^2) which may be independent or terraced, and independent factory/distribution units (15,000 ft^2 or above). The accepted standard is to provide approximately 10% of the floor space fitted out to office use specification, and the rest of the space unfinished, with power, gas and water piped to the perimeter of the building.

Office

Until recently, developers were looking for an optimum width of 12–13 m (40–44 ft) and a single tenancy for the complete building. Recent developments have tended to be 14–15 m deep buildings, mechanical ventilation, and a willingness to provide a managed building where space may be leased off floor by floor. Compared with industrial space, the quality of finishes is far higher for office use (carpet, lighting, power outlets, suspended ceiling and finishes) and rentals are on average three times as high. **5b** shows a typical late 1960s speculative office shell, and its more recent counterpart, **5c**.

Scientific uses

There is a growing awareness among estate agents, developers and fund managers that new technology firms are looking for accommodation which provides a combination of office and light industrial space. Warrington New Town developed Genesis, **6**, on the Birchwood Science Park, a building shell which was specifically planned to accommodate a mixture of office and

Figure 6. Genesis, Birchwood Science Park, Warrington. A building shell designed for maximum flexibility for science and technology-based industries.

Table 5 Buildings may be classified into five categories according to the levels of specification required.
A: involving major structural alterations, additions, new services, etc
B: general repairs to fabric, additional fire escapes, fireproofing and services
C: non-structural partitions, upgrading, finishes, overhauling services
D: upgrading finishes only
E: no work required at all

The key characteristics of buildings and the functions most appropriate to each are described below:

*Figure 7.
Problems of
naturally
ventilated
speculative
office buildings.*

light industrial or laboratory uses. Similar schemes have been developed at Kembray Park, Swindon, and Linford Wood, Milton Keynes. Rentals for this space tend to be closer to office rents, as is the specification of finish.

'Second-hand' industrial and office space

During the late 1950s and early 1960s, the UK experienced a development boom. Currently a large proportion of the stock available on the market is from this period, partly due to the termination of 21-year leases. Industrial units, as in **5c**, have poor insulation and cladding may require renewal. The office stock from this period tends to have insufficient floor-to-floor height for installing air handling, limited power outlets, thin glazed façades, which suffer from solar gain,

condensation in winter, and poor heat insulation, **7**.

Redundant premises

Due to changes in demography, methods of transportation and production technology, major

Table 6 Classification of buildings according to spatial type, and factors affecting the re-use of each type.

Building type	Typical existing use of building	Characteristics	Factors affecting reuse
Small single space	Chapel Gatehouse Stables/coach house	Single storied Detached Load bearing walls Size max 100 m²	Advantages: – Space with character for specialised use – Disadvantages: – Insufficient space
Large single space	Barn Hangar Warehouse Goods shed Engine house Factory	Single storied Detached Frame or frame and perimeter wall construction Size 100 m² Floor to eaves height 5 m +	Advantages: – Flexibility of use – Ease of movement of goods Disadvantages: – Heating – Sub-division – Servicing
Small repetitive spaces	House Housing Workshops Lock-up garages	Up to four storied Terraced Narrow frontage Up to 100 m² on each floor	Advantages: – Sub-divided for small units of accommodation Disadvantages: – Means of escape – Accessibility – Load on upper floors – Fire protection
Large repetitive spaces	Railway arches Warehouse Factory Mill	Multi-storied Deep space Frame and perimeter wall Structure size up to 3000 m² on each floor	Advantages: – Flexibility of use – Suitable for open plan multiple use Disadvantages: – Difficulty of sub-dividing into small units – Means of escape – Access – Natural light – Fire protection
Small and large spaces	Church Town hall Hospital School Industrial complex Exchange	Up to four storied Detached Mixed structural system, varying floor to ceiling heights	Advantages: – Falling vacant in key inner city sites – Well serviced, range of spaces provided (suitable for mixed uses) Disadvantages: – Complex building forms – Heating – Internal circulation of goods

shifts have occurred in the economic fortunes of parts of the country, leaving empty or underutilised buildings. Many of these buildings are well constructed, provide generous space and, with imagination, can be adapted for use by small firms. Some of the more formidable constraints to be overcome are poor accessibility, the cost of meeting statutory requirements, and the sheer size of the buildings.

However, the variety of old buildings with potential that are available (Table 6) and the growing number of developers who are more prepared to adapt some of these buildings for multi-tenancy uses, **8**, suggests that any firm looking for accommodation should not immediately rule out the option of an older building.

Use Class Categories

To control town development, planning use

*Figure 8.
An increasing number of buildings are being converted for use by several independent firms, 5 Dryden Street, Covent Garden, was converted for a working community of design practices.*

11

classes are applied to sites and buildings. These classes broadly categorise land use into heavy industrial, light industrial, and office and commercial. Table 7 provides a more exact categorisation into the relevant classes. Traditionally, planning zoning separated uses into geographical zones, the commercial centre, residential districts and industrial estates. Today, however, well established expectations about where firms wish to locate are being eroded, and the separation of office from factory and factory from laboratory is disintegrating. In order to achieve their natural pattern of work, many firms are prepared to rent office space and use it for demonstration, light industrial, storage or training purposes. Similarly, firms are, despite office planning constraints, leasing inappropriate industrial space and adapting it (often at considerable expense) for use as office, laboratory or high quality equipment space.

The whole question of use classes as they apply to the mixture of functions found in the new information based industries is at present under discussion, and firms may expect a sympathetic hearing from most planning authorities if they require a wide mix of uses.

Choosing the Most Suitable Building Shell

The range of buildings potentially available for a firm spans a wide spectrum. The choice of the most suitable shell for its activities will ensure an effective use of space and so a reduction in rental, as well as minimise fitting-out costs. Table 8 identifies the main questions to be asked about the requirements of the firm and matches those to the questions to be answered about the building shell.

Having acquired a building or unit, the process of fitting it out to meet the firm's requirement begins.

Table 7 Use classes under the Town and Country Planning Act (Use Classes) Order 1987.

Class	Uses	Notes
A1	Shops	Including post offices, ticket agencies, travel agencies, sandwich bars, hairdressers, undertakers and hire shops.
A2	Financial and professional services	Provided to visiting public.
A3	Food and drink	Sale for consumption on premises, or hot food to take away
B1	Business	Offices not in Class A2, research and development, light industry
B2	General industrial	Any industry not in Classes B1 or B3-B7
B3-B7	Special industrial groups A to E	
B8	Storage or distribution	
C1	Hotels and hostels	Including boarding and guest houses
C2	Residential institutions	Including hospitals, nursing homes, residential schools and colleges
C3	Dwelling houses	
D1	Non-residential institutions	Including health centres, creches, day schools, galleries, museums, libraries, public halls, churches
D2	Assembly and leisure	Including cinemas, concert halls, swimming baths, gymnasiums, sports fields, etc

---

Table 8 The organisation must answer a number of questions about itself which will be reflected in the building requirements.

The organisation	The building
How big?	Size of building
What technology?	Kind of servicing
What relationships?	Shape of building Number of floors
What groupings?	Percentage of small rooms Depth of building
How rapidly changing?	Flexibility Window and ceiling grids
What contact with the outside world?	Quality of finishes Number of entrances
What corporate values?	Quality of finishes

PART 2

The Process

Planning the Fitting-Out Programme

Confronted with an empty building shell, how does one set about preparing for move in? During the period of selecting space many requirements will already have been discussed and agreed with both staff and outside consultants, e.g. architect. Decisions in principle will have been made on the:
— Amount of space required (Table 9).
— Allocation of space to different functions.
— Space required for special equipment.
— Additional demands on services.
— Number and location of cellular offices.
— Quality of finish required.
Subsequent steps between acquiring the space and moving in will be to:
● Identify requirements in greater detail.
● Draw up a block plan identifying the location of functions, special equipment support functions, access points and areas demanding additional servicing.
● Decide on a specification and budget costs.
● Sketch layout plan, with specification of fitting-out work required.
● Choose the method of undertaking the fitting-out work.
● Detail design.
● Implementation.

Identifying the Costs

Rules of thumb on how much it might cost to fit out a building are almost impossible to set down. For a job over 200 m^2, it is recommended that professional advice be sought, while for smaller jobs estimates might be sought from builders or sub-contractors. The basis of any costing exercise is to identify the main jobs or elements (e.g. partitions, floor finish, etc) and assess a budget cost for each of these items (see Table 10). *Spons' Guide*, which sets down unit rates for materials and trade, is also useful for undertaking such an exercise.
The cost of fitting-out a space will be influenced by:

Condition and configuration

The condition and configuration of the building shell to be fitted out. A speculative office building will have lights, suspended ceiling and carpet as part of the basic specification, whereas an industrial unit, although a cheaper rent, will not have floor finishes, lighting or finishes included. Costs may vary depending on:
— Size of space and number of floors.
— Shape of space and floor heights.
— Window area.

Location

This will affect the rates of pay, and inaccessible areas may have a delivery premium for materials. Units on the top floor of a building or with problems of delivery parking may reflect higher building costs.

Type of layout

For office uses costs may vary depending on whether the space is open planned or cellular. The above will affect:
— Internal partitions and screens.
— Wall finishes.
— Internal doors.
— Light switching, socket outlets.
— Air handling.
Although open plan may reduce the cost of building work, it may entail additional furniture costs.

Types of activities

The functions being performed will affect:
— Amount and type of services.
— Specification of finishes.
— Amount of built-in equipment (fume cupboards, security systems, etc).

Density of staff

Tenancies with high densities of staff suggest a higher quality of specification and the need for lavatories, break area facilities and 'front office' functions.

Method of undertaking the building work

Reductions in fitting-out costs can be achieved by the client opting to do work himself or to manage rent contracts direct, so reducing main contractors' preliminaries and profits. Costs can rapidly increase, if to reduce disruption it is decided to use weekend or out of hours labour.

Getting the Work Done

The best way of undertaking the building work will depend on the amount to be done, its complexity, the speed with which it needs to be completed, the amount of time it will take and the skills available within the company.
Once the decision has been made to occupy a building the pressure will be on to move in as soon as possible to reduce the payment of unnecessary rent.

On deciding to move, review the work required and divide it into three categories:
— Essential work which must be completed before occupation because it is disruptive. This will include structural and wet trades, which may be noisy, smelly, dirty or require the movement of materials.
— Work that would preferably be done before moving in, but could be undertaken during occupancy, e.g. erecting partitions, electrics and decorating.

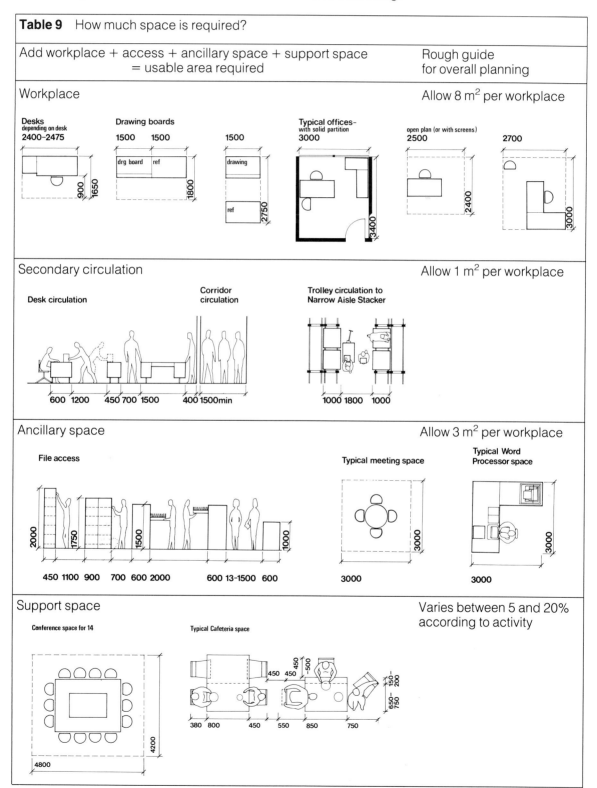

Table 9 How much space is required?

Add workplace + access + ancillary space + support space = usable area required — Rough guide for overall planning

Workplace — Allow 8 m² per workplace

Secondary circulation — Allow 1 m² per workplace

Ancillary space — Allow 3 m² per workplace

Support space — Varies between 5 and 20% according to activity

— Work that could be done after the move-in with little disruption, e.g. external decoration, specialist areas that can be closed off.

The decision about the amount of work to undertake before moving in will be influenced by cash flow, the degree to which the firm's business and staff can cope with disruption and the length of rent-free period it is possible to negotiate. In today's economic climate it is possible to negotiate 6–9 months rent free. Do not underestimate the disruption to staff concentration and the inconvenience to visitors and customers that such things as hammering or the ever-present smell of glue can cause. The extra cost of completing essential building work may be a small price to pay against a fall-off in business and the loss of valued staff. The procedure for fitting out will vary depending on whether the firm is moving into a new building still under construction, or into an existing building.

Fitting out a new building

By negotiating early with the developer, the firm may be able to influence the final specification of finishes, adjust services to meet their specialist requirements, and rentalise additional work they require. By overlapping with the existing contract and using the existing professionals and contractors, considerable savings may be made on money and time. In negotiating leasehold improvements with the developer, the firm should appoint its own professionals to liaise with the developer's professionals and safeguard its interests.

Alterations and adaptations to existing buildings

Structural adaptations and the upgrading of the fabric may well be required. Invaluable information and the original plans may be available from the original architect, builder or in the District Surveyor's office. For small jobs where structural alterations are required the District Surveyor must be consulted and can be a valuable source of advice. Changes of access, additional sub-division and change of use would be confirmed with the Fire Officer.

In choosing the method of getting the work done, time may be more important than cost. Working around activities already in the building, or using ad hoc contracting procedure, although seemingly cheaper, may take far longer than predicted and result in extra, and increased, costs through inflation, interest payments and opportunity costs.

Contractual Procedures

As a firm, there are four ways that you may decide to organise the fitting-out contract:
— By undertaking the work yourself.
— By employing skills direct, and entering into direct contracts with suppliers.
— By employing a main contactor, who then organises suppliers and sub-contractors.

— By appointing professionals, e.g. an architect or surveyor, who will then design, specify and manage the building work on your behalf.

Each of these forms of contractual procedures have their advantages and drawbacks.

Doing it yourself

While at first glance this looks to save the profits of others and gain the purchasing discounts for material direct, it will use valuable staff time which might be better employed in nurturing the growth of the business. Do-it-yourself becomes worthwhile for simple, small jobs where members of the firm are prepared to give their evenings and weekends over to fitting-out work in the form of 'sweat equity'. Even if it is a small job, a professional architect or surveyor's advice on an hourly rate of payment could be invaluable at the early stages of planning the space, deciding on the opportunities, and specifying the work to be done and components to be used.

Acting as main contractor

In this case you can use your managerial and purchasing skills to organise outside labour. Although more expensive than doing the work yourself, you will avoid inefficiences and the 'learning curve' will be saved by using skilled labour. Other savings are on main contractor's overheads, profits on labour and preliminary costs and professional fees. These savings should be set against your own staff time, the rental of specialised equipment, and the main contractor's or professional's experience of supervising and negotiating with sub-contractors. For those firms which decide to use their in-house purchasing and supervision skills, the use of an outside professional to provide a limited service can bring a wider knowledge of competitive pricing, specification and project management. These skills can be used to supplement and supervise your in-house staff.

Using a main contractor

On paper, this is the most expensive approach, but real savings can be made by undertaking the work more efficiently, getting it done more quickly, and, if all goes smoothly, the work will be completed to a high quality, with the minimum worry to yourself, leaving you to run your business.

Using professionals, or specialised service firms

For larger jobs this method means that you benefit from the professional's previous experience. An independent adviser looks after your interests and, having agreed a brief, the work will be carried out efficiently and at competitive prices on your behalf. The professional, architect, engineer or surveyor can contribute to the fitting-out process in a variety of ways:

Figure 9.
RIBA Architect's
Appointment.
Range of
services
provided.

Partial services

SW4.15 The architect may be required to provide part only of the Basic Services (Part 1). In such cases the architect will be entitled to a commensurate fee. All percentage fees for partial services shall be based on the architect's current estimate of the total construction cost of the works.

— Limited consultancy: where the professional provides skilled advice for the client to act upon. This is probably in the form of an extended letter, short report, or sketches and is paid for on an hourly or day rate, or as a lump sum for providing the advice.
This sort of involvement can be of tremendous value to the client, remunerative to the professional, and cost both sides the minimum of time for the maximum effect.
— Partial services: where the professional provides the relevant services out of the complete range he would expect to offer under his full service, as set down in the R I B A Architect's appointment, **9**. The client may well wish to use the architect's planning and design skills in agreeing the type and quality of work to be done, but to undertake the supervision and management of the contract himself, accepting the rules attached.
For partial services, fees may be charged on an

hourly rate, as a lump sum agreed in advance, or as a percentage of the estimated or final construction costs.
— Full service: each of the professional bodies sets out recommended conditions of engagement, and work stages. The full architect's service is outlined in **10**, with the suggested input as a percentage of the total work. The professional bodies recommend that this work is paid for as a percentage of the final building cost, the percentage varying depending on the value of the project and whether it is new-building or conversion work.
— Emerging roles: a growing number of architectural and surveying firms, realising the attraction of a 'one stop' fixed price service to the client, are providing an extended service. This service could include managing all the professionals and sub-contractors on the client's behalf and guaranteeing a fixed price subject to an outline specification. Fees would be negotiated on a lump sum, percentage, or 'by performance' basis. 'By performance' is a scheme whereby the fee increases in proportion to the saving on the final contract sum. This considers the concern of clients who feel uneasy at the way the professional's fee increases as building costs escalate.

Figure 10.
RIBA Architect's
Appointment.
Scope of full
architect's
service.

Part 1
Architect's services

This part describes Preliminary and Basic Services which an architect will normally provide. These services progress through work stages based on the RIBA Plan of Work (RIBA Publications Ltd).

PRELIMINARY SERVICES

Work stages A and B: Inception and feasibility

SW1.1   Discuss the client's requirements; assess these and give general advice on how to proceed.

SW1.2   Advise on any need for specialist contractors, sub-contractors or suppliers.

SW1.3   Carry out such preparatory work as may be necessary to determine the feasibility of the client's requirements.

BASIC SERVICES

Work stages C and D: Outline proposals and scheme design

SW1.4   Prepare outline proposals and develop a scheme design; prepare a cost estimate; where applicable give an indication of possible start and completion dates for the building contract.

SW1.5   Make where required application for planning permission. (n.b. The permission itself is beyond the architect's control and no guarantee that it will be granted can be given.)

Work stage E: Detail design

SW1.6   Develop the scheme design; co-ordinate any work of specialist contractors, sub-contractors or suppliers.

SW1.7   Carry out cost checks as necessary; advise on the consequences of any subsequent changes on the cost and programme.

SW1.8   Make and negotiate where required applications for approvals under building acts, regulations or other statutory requirements.

Work stages F and G: Production information

SW1.9   Prepare production information including drawings, schedules and specification of materials and workmanship in sufficient detail to enable a contractor to prepare a tender.

Work stages H, J, K and L: Tender to completion

SW1.10   Invite tenders from approved contractors; advise on tenders submitted. Alternatively arrange for a price to be negotiated with a contractor.

SW1.11   Advise on the appointment of the contractor; where required prepare the building contract and arrange for it to be signed by the client and the contractor.

SW1.12   Administer the terms of the building contract; visit the site as appropriate to inspect generally the progress and quality of the work; make where required periodic financial reports to the client.

SW1.13   Administer the terms of the building contract relating to the completion of the works; give general guidance on maintenance; provide a set of drawings showing the building and the main lines of drainage.

Figure 11.
Typical office
building.
a) Plan.
b) Section for
which costs
have been
estimated
and shown on
Table 12.

Specification and Budget Costs

In order to compare the costs of varying the specification, costs of components at basic, medium and high levels of specification have been estimated for a typical light industrial unit, **11**, and a typical office unit, **12**. (The light industrial user has been assumed to have 20% of the area used as office and a staff occupancy of twenty.)

Table 10 outlines a basic, medium and high specification for each component, e.g. Partitions, Screens.

Table 11 gives the costs of each of these components at basic, medium and high specification, presented as an average cost per

ft^2 of gross floor area. A worked example, using these tables to achieve a total cost, plus total cost per m^2/GFA, is shown in Table 12.

As can be seen from this table, the most sensitive elements in office installation costs are:

The most critical elements in the fitting out of a typical light industrial unit are:
— Mezzanine floors 15% of floor area.
— Internal sub-division.
— Floor finishes.
— Lighting.
— Power supply.

The specification in the light industrial unit will be lower and it is assumed that structure and servicing systems can be exposed.

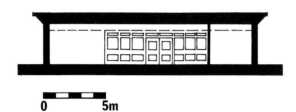

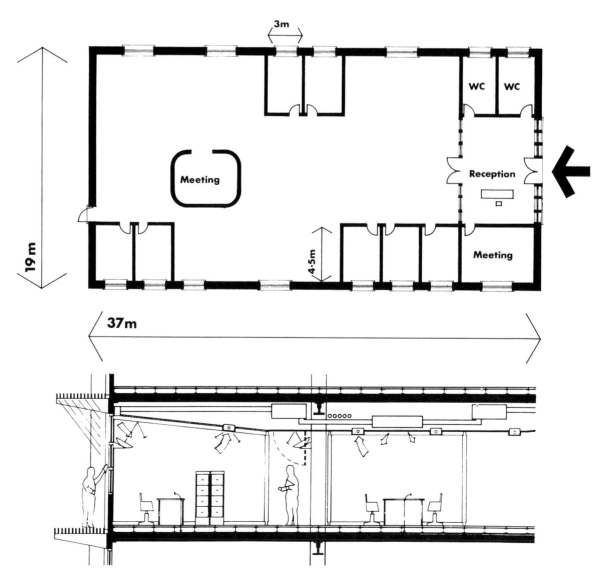

Figure 12.
Typical light industrial building.
a) Plans.
b) Section for which costs have been estimated and shown on Table 9.

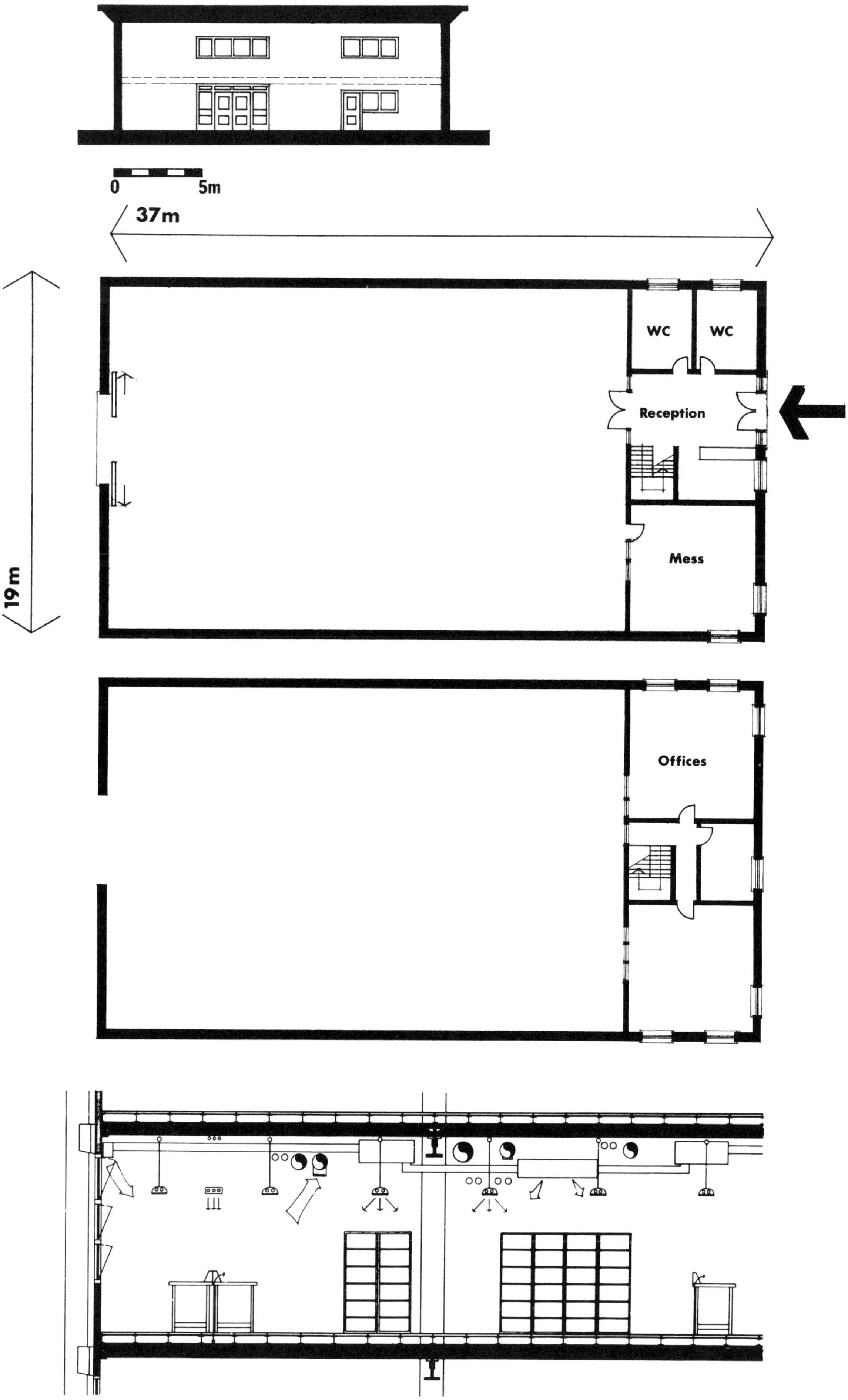

37m

19m

0   5m

WC   WC

Reception

Mess

Offices

Table 10
Brief
specification of
works –
component
guide.

Table 10 Brief specification of works – component guide.			
Element	**Basic**	**Medium**	**High**
Building Component			
Internal partitions/ doors	Plastered blockwork/ studwork walls Solid core doors	Self-finished demountable partitions solid/glazed Glazed/solid doors	As medium but with higher acoustic performance and more flexibility
Suspended ceilings	Plasterboard and skim	Regular fibre tile on concealed grid	Acoustic perforated metal
Floors – raised access		Chipboard on softwood bearers	Fully accessible tiles on adjustable metal legs
Solar control – external	Retractable awnings	Fixed vertical solar control screen of solid construction	Electrically operated adjustable louvred screens
Building Services			
Power supply – trunking (excludes mains supplies)	Perimeter skirting trunking plus power to columns/overhead bus bar	Underfloor trunking at regular intervals	As medium but with additional service poles and perimeter dado trunking
Lighting (excludes mains supplies)	Lay in twin fluorescent fitting 1 per 19 m^2 with opal diffuser	Upgrade basic at 1 per 6 m^2 and with anti-glare diffusers	Range of different lighting general/ directional/local
Fire protection	Manual fire alarm/fire extinguishers	Automatic heat sensory equipment/ hose reels	Automatic sprinklers
Plumbing – toilets and water supply	Individual sanitary fittings	Pre-plumbed sanitaryware	Self-contained prefabricated toilet unit
Water heating	Single instantaneous heater	Multipoint heaters	Indirect cylinder
Ventilation – air extraction	Ventilation grilles in window frames/roof ventilators	Extract fans in windows	Heat recovery recirculating fans plus ventilation to central and special areas
Ventilation – heating, cooling conditioning	Ducted warm air system which can also be used for ventilation	Through the wall AC units	Full air-conditioning ducted or fan coil units with central chiller
Heating	Electric night storage heaters	Low pressure hot water system with radiators	Low pressure hot water system with fan assisted heaters
Independent Components			
Screens – heavy duty	Freestanding metal faced with doors, etc	Freestanding metal or plasterboard forming enclosed areas	As Medium but upgraded acoustic performance and includes range of finishes and accessories
Screens – light duty	Freestanding fabric covered to enclose workstations	Freestanding linked/ combination screens sound absorbent	As Medium but upgraded acoustic performance and includes range of finishes and accessories
Floor finishes	Carpet tiles/vinyl sheeting	80:20 carpet/hard wearing non-slip finish	As Medium but upgraded finish
Mezzanine floor	Single open grid/ timber flooring basic handrail	Metal open grid deck/ handrail Enclosed deck	Enclosed deck

Materials handling/lifting equipment	Dock leveller	Elevating dock/scissor lift	Dock leveller and goods lift
External elements	Exposed dustbin/cycle shelter	Enclosed shelters	As Medium but upgraded specification

Independent Services

Security	Window locks/single alarm	Full detection system	As Medium but upgraded specification
Communications systems	1 telephone per 40 m^2 of offices/PMBX/Intercom, etc (amortised over 5 years)	1 telephone per 30 m^2 of offices Intercom (amortised over 5 years)	1 telephone per 20 m^2 of offices Monarch System/Telex/Fax/Intercom (amortised over 5 years)

Furniture, Fittings and Accessories

Furniture – office systems	Independent units may be part of a system	Coordinated range	Coordinated range including screens wire management and task lighting
Office storage	Softwood/metal shelves/filing cabinets	Metal storage/filing system part of a range	Lateral cabinet system/plan storage, etc
Special furniture and fittings	Independent units may be part of a system	Coordinated range including additional accessories	As Medium but upgraded specification
Industrial and scientific systems fittings and storage	Independent units may be part of a system	Coordinated range including trolleys, etc	As Medium but upgraded specification
Solar control – internal	Paper blinds	Venetian blinds/curtains	Special solar control thin bladed Venetian blinds
Signage	Strategic only (access/company)	Access/company/department	Access/company/department/individual

Table 11
Summary of
component
costs.

Table 11 Summary of component costs, £/m² gross floor area.

| Element | Offices (Assuming 929 m² GFA – see note below) | | | | Comment |
	Basic £/m² GFA	Medium £/m² GFA	High £/m² GFA	Average £/m² GFA	
Building Component					
Internal partitions/doors	38.75	53.80	65.70	52.70	40% cellularisation
Suspended ceilings	10.80	17.20	26.90	18.30	100% area
Floors – raised access	–	21.50	37.70	29.60	100% area
Solar control – external	6.45	8.60	10.80	8.60	One side only
Building Services					
Power supply – trunking	14.00	21.50	30.10	21.50	Excludes mains supply
Lighting	12.90	19.40	26.90	19.90	Excludes mains supply
Fire protection	2.15	4.30	16.10	7.50	Excludes mains water supply
Plumbing – toilets and water supply	4.80	5.90	7.00	5.90	Excludes drainage and mains water supplies
Water heating	1.10	1.60	2.15	1.60	–
Ventilation – air extraction	1.60	3.20	10.80	5.40	–
Ventilation – heating, cooling, conditioning	16.10	38.75	129.20	61.35	100% area
Heating	13.45	21.50	26.90	20.45	Gas fired system
Independent Components					
Screens – heavy duty	–	–	–	–	–
Screens – light duty	18.30	30.70	36.60	28.50	40 staff in open area
Floor finishes	12.90	19.40	23.70	18.80	100% area
Mezzanine floors	–	–	–	–	–
Materials handling/lifting equipment	–	–	–	–	–
External elements	6.45	9.70	12.90	20.45	Bin enclosure
Independent Services					
Security	3.20	6.45	8.10	5.90	–
Communications systems	2.15	3.20	5.40	3.80	Monarch System – amortised over 5 years
Furniture, Fittings and Accessories					
Furniture – office system	59.20	96.90	153.90	103.30	50No. complete workstations
Office storage	23.10	38.75	59.20	40.40	Filing, etc, 50No. people
Special furniture and fittings	21.50	32.30	43.05	32.30	Reception/meetings, etc
Industrial and scientific fittings and storage	–	–	–	–	–
Solar control – internal	2.15	3.20	5.40	3.80	All windows
Signage	1.60	3.20	7.50	3.80	–

Table 11 Summary of component costs, £/m² gross floor area.

| Element | Light Industrial (Assuming 929m² GFA – see note below) | | | | Comment |
	Basic £/m² GFA	Medium £/m² GFA	High £/m² GFA	Average £/m² GFA	
Building Component					
Internal partitions/doors	18.30	23.70	26.90	23.10	Reception/offices approx 20% of floor area
Suspended ceilings	3.20	5.40	8.10	5.40	Reception/offices approx 20% of floor area
Floors – raised access	–	–	–	–	
Solar control – external	4.80	6.45	8.60	6.45	Gable end only
Building Services					
Power supply – trunking	11.80	19.40	24.75	18.80	Excludes mains supply
Lighting	10.80	17.20	23.70	17.20	Excludes mains supply
Fire protection	1.60	4.30	15.10	7.00	Excludes mains water supply
Plumbing – toilets and water supply	4.80	5.90	7.00	5.90	Excludes drainage and mains water supplies
Water heating	1.10	1.60	2.15	1.60	–
Ventilation – air extraction	1.60	3.20	10.80	5.40	–
Ventilation – heating, cooling, conditioning	6.45	15.10	53.80	25.30	Reception/office areas only
Heating	10.80	18.80	24.20	17.80	Gas fired system
Independent Components					
Screens – heavy duty	6.45	8.60	10.80	8.60	Enclosing mezzanine
Screens – light duty	3.80	6.45	10.80	6.45	10 staff in open area
Floor finishes	11.80	14.00	19.40	15.10	Carpet to office areas
Mezzanine floors	10.80	16.10	23.10	16.70	15% of floor area
Materials handling/lifting equipment	5.90	16.10	37.70	19.90	Goods lift in high option
External elements	5.40	8.10	10.80	8.10	Cycle shed/bin enclosure
Independent Services					
Security	2.15	3.20	5.40	3.80	–
Communications systems	1.60	2.70	3.20	2.70	Herald System – amortised over 5 years
Furniture, Fittings and Accessories					
Furniture – office system	10.80	16.10	24.75	17.20	10No. complete workstations
Office storage	3.80	9.10	12.90	8.60	10No. people
Special furniture and fittings	9.70	13.45	16.10	12.90	Reception/mess room
Industrial and scientific fittings and storage	14.50	24.75	37.70	25.80	40No. operatives
Solar control – internal	1.10	1.60	2.15	1.60	Offices only
Signage	1.10	1.60	2.15	1.60	–

Notes:
(See worked example)
The indicative costs listed above are current as at 2nd quarter 1986 and are mutually *inclusive* of main contractors' profits, overheads and site preliminaries and assume that:
1a. The office project will be approximately 929m² GFA in size, accommodating 70 people and with a total contract value *excluding* furniture of approximately £200,000 or £215/m² GFA.
1b. The light industrial project will be approximately 929m² GFA in size, accommodating 40 people and with a total contract value *excluding* furniture of approximately £130,000 or £140/m² GFA.
2. The project will be undertaken in south-east England.
3. The works will be let on a full competitive tender basis.
4. There will be full design team involvement.
The costs *exclude* any allowances for:
1. Professional fees.
2. VAT.
3. Inflation.

Table12
Worked
example, taking
into account
size, contract
procurement,
regional location
and fees.

Table 12   Worked example.

	Offices (See Fig. 11)		Light Industrial (See Fig. 12)	
	Gross floor area: 650.3 m²		Gross floor area: 817.5 m²	
	Staff: 50No		Staff:	
			Office: 10No	
			Production: 25No	
	Cellularisation: 20%		Percentage office/industrial: 15%	
	Location: South-east		Location: North-east	
	Contract: Conventional		Contract: Design and build	
	Contract period: 22–24 weeks		Contract period: 18–20 weeks	
	Fees: Full service		Fees: Partial service	

Element	Offices £/m² GFA	Quality	Light industrial £/m² GFA	Quality
Building Component				
Internal partitions/doors	32.30*	Medium *(20% cellular)	18.30	Basic
Suspended ceilings	17.20	Medium	5.40	Medium
Floors – raised access	21.50	Medium	–	–
Solar control – external	8.60	Medium	4.80	Basic
Building Services				
Power supply – trunking	21.50	Medium	11.80	Basic
Lighting	26.90	High	10.80	Basic
Fire protection	2.15	Basic	15.00	High
Plumbing – toilets and water supply	4.80	Basic	7.00	High
Water heating	2.15	High	1.00	Basic
Ventilation – air extraction	10.80	High	10.80	High
Ventilation – heating, cooling conditioning	38.75	Medium	N/A	–
Heating	N/A	–	10.80	Basic
Independent Components				
Screens – heavy duty	N/A	–	8.60	Medium
Screens – light duty	30.70	Medium	6.45	Medium
Floor finishes	19.40	Medium	11.80	Basic
Mezzanine floors	N/A	–	16.10	Medium
Materials handling/lifting equipment	N/A	–	5.90	Basic
External elements	6.45	Basic	8.00	Medium
Independent Services				
Security	3.20	Basic	5.40	High
Communications systems	5.40	High	1.60	Basic
Furniture, Fittings and Accessories				
Furniture – office system	96.90	Medium	10.80	Basic
Office storage	38.75	Medium	3.80	Basic
Special furniture and fittings	32.30	Medium	13.45	Medium
Industrial and scientific fittings and storage	N/A	–	24.75	Medium
Solar control – internal	3.20	Medium	1.00	Basic
Signage	7.50	High	1.60	Medium
Contingencies				
10% design and construction contingencies	43.05		21.50	
	———————		———————	
	974/m² GFA × 650.3 m²		237/m² GFA × 817.5 m²	
	———————		———————	
	£308,000		£193,000	

Weighting adjustments		
Contract size		
Up to 278.7 m²	×12.90	×12.90
278.7–929 m²	×10.80	×10.80
Over 929 m²	× 9.70	× 9.70
	=£308,000	=£193,000
Regional location		
North-east	× 9.50	× 9.50
Midlands/South-west	× 9.60	× 9.60
Wales/Scotland	× 9.70	× 9.70
Southern/Home Counties	×10.20	×10.20
South-east	×10.80	×10.80
	=£308,000	£169,000
Contract procurement		
Client acting as main contractor	× 9.70	× 9.70
Design and build	×10.20	×10.20
Fee management	×10.40	×10.40
Conventional tender	×10.80	×10.80
	=£308,000	=£160,000
Professional fees (full design team)		
Limited consultancy	+6%	+6%
Partial services	+10%	+10%
Full consultancy	+14%	+14%
TOTAL COST	=£350,000	=£176,000
	or 538.21/m² GFA	or 215.28/m² GFA

Note:
The above costs are current as at 2nd Quarter 1986 but *exclude* any allowances for:

1. VAT.
2. Interest charges.
3. Acquisition costs.
4. Inflation.
5. Machinery and equipment.
6. Data cabling.

Learning from Experience

How do small firms adapt existing buildings to their specific requirements? Examples of their resourcefulness are shown in the following eight case studies.

The studies have been selected from locations which range from a turn-of-the century converted grain warehouse to a modern industrial unit on a New Town estate. The eight firms varied from professional office orientated organisations and high technology electronic firms to a small picture framing company.

Table 13 (p.27) summarises the characteristics of the firms, their accommodation, and the way they approached the fitting out.

Firms tended to invest money in the equipment for the production process and staff, rather than in adapting premises. Fitting out tended to be modest, with a good deal of the work being undertaken by the founders of the firm themselves in the evening or at weekends. Sometimes this work was quite substantial, using basic materials such as wood and plasterboard which could be bought from the local builders' merchant and cut to size, or dexion slats which could be bolted together to make storage area and room dividers.

The new industrial units in the Development Corporations provided a higher level of servicing, with the Development Corporation providing professional support in adapting or adding additional services, as required. The new industrial units were unable to compete with the robustness of the pre-1940s buildings, and there were frequent comments about poor insulation, leaks, poor durability and maintenance, and the fragile nature of the construction.

Table 13
Summary of
case studies.

Table 13	Summary of case studies						
Firm	Location	Type of shell	Size of organisation	Method of fitting out	Use of professionals	Amount of fitting out	Services added
FIRM A Architects	Central London	Refurbished 1920s Industrial	35 staff 650 m²	Professional builder Phased cost plus contact	Architect/QS	Structural work to shell, scenery, services	Lighting, toilets, electrical trunking, upgrade heating
FIRM B Quantity Surveyors	Central London	Refurbished 1920s Industrial	12 staff 240 m²	Professional builder Fixed price contract	Full professional services	High quality scenery, services and furniture	Lighting, hot water, localised AC
FIRM C Makers and distributors of video cassettes	Outer London	Adapted 1930s multi-storeyed industrial building	4 staff 100 m²	DIY at weekends and evenings Gradual	None	Scenery, services, stud partitions suspended ceiling	Electric fan heater, rewiring, new lighting Kitchenette
FIRM D Importers and distributors of picture frames	Outer London	Adapted 1930s multi-storeyed industrial building	7 staff 200 m²	DIY	None	Scenery, services, stud partitions Industrial shelving New doors	Local electric heating Water heating and sink unit Localised fans
FIRM E Graphic designer, printing and photographic services	City fringe London	Adapted nineteenth-century multi-storeyed industrial building	2 staff 30 m²	DIY	None	Scenery, services, stud partitions, furniture	Electric fan heaters, lighting, electrical trunking New sink and darkroom plumbing
FIRM F Computer Consultancy supplying systems and software	City fringe London	Adapted nineteenth-century multi-storeyed industrial building	4 staff 36 m²	DIY Electrical contractors	None	Scenery, services, furniture	Bar heaters, lighting, electrical trunking
FIRM G Architects	Industrial estate, Warrington	1980s adapted industrial shed	15 staff 350 m²	Professional builder	Architect Full professional services	New mezzanine block partitions, new stair Scenery, services and furniture	Lighting, electrical trunking, heating, blinds, kitchen
FIRM H Design and manufacture of micro-processor-based systems	Industrial estate, Milton Keynes	1975 'advanced factory unit'	6 staff 280 m²	DIY	None	Scenery, services, block partition, new steel mezzanine and stairs	Lighting

27

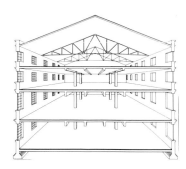

Character and style through careful choice of scenery

Firm A Date of occupancy 1981	Architects and space planners Architectural and design practice specialising in office planning, briefing and re-use of redundant buildings, employing approximately 35 staff
Building prior to move-in (shell-related)	
Second-hand industrial and office premises built *c.* 1920 Comprises five floors within a concrete frame, and r.c. slab structure with brick infill Floor width 20 m, floor height 3 m Firm A occupy basement to first floor inclusive, giving a leaseable area of 650 m^2	Existing electricity, water and telephones distributed internally Existing oil-fired boiler Toilets provided on each floor Lift provided
Building components and services after move-in (shell-related)	
New internal stud partition to basement and ground floors Artex to finish to underside of slab New entrance lobby New woodblock flooring to basement	Power supply redistributed New uplighters and downlighters to basement and ground floor areas New plumbing to kitchen and toilet areas New fittings to some areas Existing low pressure hot water radiators Natural ventilation New telephone main frame in basement
Independent components and services after move-in (scenery-related)	
New heavy duty fixed screens and shelving Ground floor re-carpeted, first floor existing carpets	New entrance sign Task lighting (Anglepoise) Purpose-made perimeter worktops combined with re-used furniture and storage units Photocopier, telex and word-processor equipment New Monarch PABX installed
General comments	
Medium price range office refit which maintains the industrial character of the building exterior	Contract for refurbishment let to firm of shopfitters

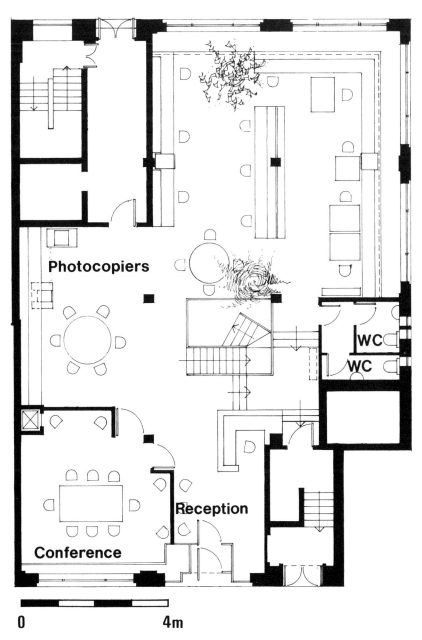

Photocopiers

WC

WC

Conference

Reception

0   4m

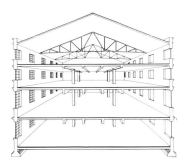

Enhancing the appearance with shell-related components

Firm B	Quantity Surveyors
Date of occupancy 1982	Preparation of bills of quantities
	Employs 12 staff

Building prior to move-in (shell-related)

Second-hand industrial and office premises built *c.* 1920 Comprises five floors within a concrete frame, and r.c. slab structure with brick infill Floor width 20 m, floor height 3 m The firm occupies the second and third floors, giving a lettable area of 240 m ^{2}	Existing electricity, water and telephones distributed internally Existing oil-fired boiler Toilets provided on each floor Lift provided

Building components and services after move-in (shell-related)

New internal stud partitions between floor and structural slab New suspended ceilings (proprietory system) installed Floors untouched	Power supply re-routed into worktop height trunking Integrated fluorescent ceiling lights New plumbing to new kitchen, existing toilets refurbished Electric water heater Natural ventilation Existing low pressure hot water radiators New localised AC system

Independent components and services after move-in (scenery-related)

Purpose-made heavy duty fixed screens Demountable panel and shelf system at central workstations and library New carpet installed Photocopying and word-processor equipment Nameplate positioned outside tenant space	Task lighting (Anglepoise) New 'Herald' telephone exchange system and telex Purpose-made worktops lining perimeter throughout (melamine finish) Open metal shelving, 'standard' filing (second-hand) cabinets, purpose-made shelving lining perimeter of work areas

General comments

High quality interior refit which did not affect external industrial appearance of building exterior	Full professional services employed in design and refitting

```
                              Workspace    Office
                    Reception
    Store   Computer                       Workspace
    Photocopy        Library
    & Files                                WC
                                           WC
    Workspace   Workspace
```

0   4m

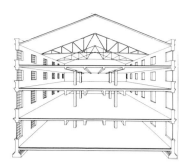

Office image in a factory environment

Firm C Date of occupancy 1979	Video and Cassette products Transferring of film to video format and duplication of video cassettes Employs 4 staff
Building prior to move-in (shell-related)	
Multi-storey factory complex built *c.* 1920 Renovated and divided into 65 tenant units in 1977. Comprises six lettable floors within a concrete frame, and r.c. slab structure with concrete block infill Floor width approximately 17 m, floor height 4.6 m Twentieth-Century Video Ltd occupies one unit on the second floor with a lettable area of 100 m² New 3 m deep open access gallery within exterior walls at courtyard	Existing electricity, telephone lines to building, cold water provided to perimeter of unit Existing gas-fired hot air heater provided Male and female toilets provided in each unit Three staircases, four goods lifts and one passenger lift within the building
Building components and services after move-in (shell-related)	
Installation of stud partitions throughout unit New system suspended over all areas except duplicating room Cleaning and costing of existing r.c. slab Signage at entrance to commercial centre and at unit entrance	Power supply rewired and distributed along perimeter and via new dropped ceiling New concealed lights and downlights Installation of kitchenette New electric water heater Ventilation by fans at present, AC system planned for future. Security system installed (burglar alarm)
Independent components and services after move-in (scenery-related)	
New felt-backed carpet Television monitors, broadcast machines, tele-cine machine, various videos recording equipment	Vertical blinds on reception area window Equipment racking throughout Tenant installed telephone line to existing hook- up New electric fan heaters
General comments	
Low price range do-it-yourself office and workroom refit – domestic scale internally; external image industrial	Tenants avail themselves of each others' services Community centre has live-in caretaker as security measure

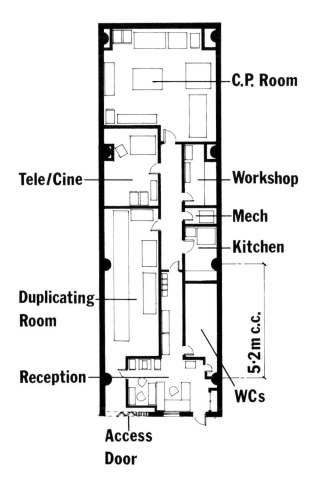

C.P. Room

Tele/Cine

Workshop

Mech

Kitchen

Duplicating
Room

5·2 m c.c.

Reception

WCs

Access
Door

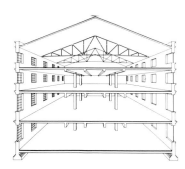

Upgrading the existing industrial character with a minimum budget

Firm D Date of occupancy 1981	Importers and Distributors Picture and photo frame importers concentrating on products from West Germany Employs 7 staff
Building prior to move-in (shell-related)	
Multi-storey factory complex built c. 1920 and renovated and divided into 65 tenant units in 1977 Comprises six lettable floors within a concrete frame, and r.c. slab structure with concrete infill Floor width approximately 34 m, floor height 4.6 m Frame up occupies two units on the third floor with a lettable area approximately 200 m² New 3 m deep open access gallery within exterior walls at courtyard	Existing electricity, telephone lines and cold water provided to perimeter of unit Gas-fired hot air heater provided Two toilets provided in each unit Three staircases, four goods lifts and one passenger lift within the building Natural ventilation
Building components and services after move-in (shell-related)	
Installation of stud partitions and suspended ceiling for office and reception areas, additional 3 m high trellised wood structure for vertical screening and storage above Cleaning and coating of existing r.c. slab Heavy duty folding, sliding door for access to storage area, signage at entrance to unit	Power supply distributed along perimeter and via existing suspended ceiling New overhead fluorescent lights New water heating unit and sink unit New industrial ionisers and fans from ceiling
Independent components and services after move-in (scenery-related)	
Heavy duty metal pallet shelves provide divisions in storage areas Office and reception areas carpeted, r.c. slab painted and exposed in storage area Hand-controlled forklift in storage area	Custom-made furniture for reception area, new standard or used furniture elsewhere Racks and 1.6 m overhead space for storage Vertical blinds on office and reception area windows Installation of local electric heaters in office and reception areas, connection to existing gas heater for storage
General comments	
Low price range office and industrial refit Retaining industrial character of building, both internally and externally	Two link and two independent tenant installed telephone lines Tenants avail themselves of each others' services (use next door's telex) Community centre has live-in caretaker as security measure

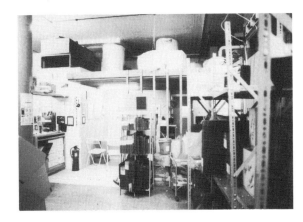

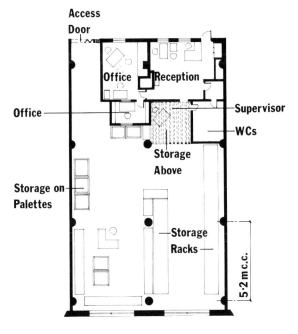

Access
Door

Office

Reception

Office

Supervisor

WCs

Storage
Above

Storage on
Palettes

Storage
Racks

5·2 m c.c.

35

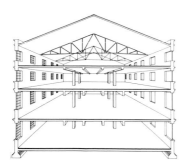

Self-help makes a workplace of character

Firm E Date of occupancy 1982	Graphic design, printing and photographic services Employs 2 staff
Building prior to move-in (shell-related)	
Rehabilitated Victorian grain warehouse comprising six floors. Cast-iron column structure with timber floors and brick walls, accommodating 40 self-contained workshops. Concrete block internal sub-division, overall width approx 30 m, with light well Floor height 3 m	Firm E occupies 30 m² on second floor Electricity, gas, water services to perimeter of unit Natural ventilation Floors block wired for telephones – up to five lines per unit Common parts include toilets, drinking water, electric light, goods and passenger lifts
Building components and services after move-in (shell-related)	
Stud partitions erected to form darkroom Ceiling and blockwork walls decorated	Ceiling mounted fluorescent lighting Power points and surface trunking Sign in entrance lobby and unit front door Plumbing and drainage to new sink unit and darkroom
Independent components and services after move-in (scenery-related)	
New carpet	Telephone installed Electric fan heaters Task lighting (Anglepoise lamps) New desks and filing cabinets Second-hand drawing boards Photographic processing equipment Offset litho machine Guillotine, stitching machines
General comments	
All work DIY	Tenants take over basic shell without finishes Tenants swap services with each other

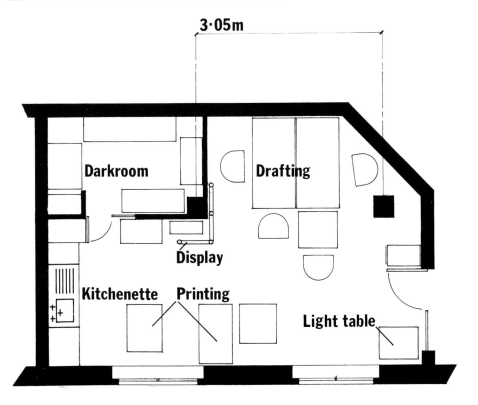

3·05m

Darkroom

Drafting

Display

Kitchenette   Printing

Light table

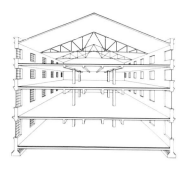

Relying on the building shell to provide the character

Firm F Date of occupancy 1982	Computer consultancy supplying systems and software. Employs 4 staff
Building prior to move-in (shell-related)	
Rehabilitated Victorian grain warehouse comprising six floors. Cast-iron column structure with timber floors and brick external walls, accommodating 40 small workshops with concrete block internal sub-division. Overall floor width approx 30 m, including light well Floor height 3 m	Firm F occupies 36 m² on third floor Electricity, gas, water services to perimeter of units Natural ventilation Floors block-wired for telephones – up to five lines available to each unit Common parts include toilets, drinking water, electric light, goods and passenger lifts
Building components and services after move-in (shell-related)	
Ceiling and blockwork walls had to be painted (5 coats)	Ceiling mounted fluorescent strip lighting Power points and surface trunking Sign in entrance lobby and at front door of unit
Independent components and services after move-in (scenery-related)	
New carpet	Telephone installed Bar fire electric heater Second-hand furniture – desks and filing cabinets New micro-computer
General comments	
Electrical work contracted out Decorations DIY	High-quality shell conversion with minimum of finishes provided for tenants Tenants avail each other of their services

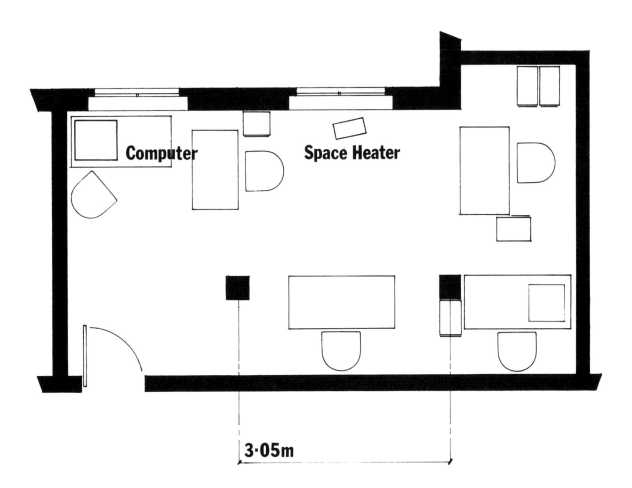

Computer

Space Heater

3·05m

Innovative adaptation of an industrial shed for creative working

Firm G Date of occupancy October 1981	Architectural firm Public and private sector work, with a recent concentration on industrial and commercial re-use of redundant buildings Employs 15 staff at Cheshire branch
Building prior to move-in (shell-related)	
1980s industrial shell adapted for office use. Single-storey steel frame structure with r.c. slab and concrete block infill faced out with corrugated metal. Ceiling height slopes from 4.5 to 6 m to eaves; front mezzanine height 2.7 – 3.1 m to eaves. Floor width 14 m. Firm G has a lettable area of 350 m²	Electric and water distributed internally Free-standing gas-fired heater at centre of shed wall Water and upper mezzanine heated by small gas-fired boiler Two toilet rooms provided One stair (two-hour rating) provided to existing mezzanine at front of space
Building components and services after move-in (shell-related)	
New load bearing concrete block walls support extension to mezzanine above and enclosed new garage space Free-standing heaters boxed-in with concrete block for noise reduction Corrugated metal roof with skylights left exposed New spiral stair to addition of upper mezzanine	New electrical trunking down flank walls and across floor via plastic section on 3 m grid Firm G used existing overhead lighting system (fixed directly on roof), with additional spotlights on roof at front area; new overhead lighting to upper mezzanine Heat produced by modified gas heater and distributed by ducting above Small gas-fire heaters modified for mezzanine above New electrically operated blind at mezzanine level for reduction of heat gain and solar control Portable AC unit for mezzanine office Natural ventilation to space below mezzanine New one-hour fire exit New kitchen installed
Independent components and services after move-in (scenery-related)	
Large concrete block planters serve as workplace screening Heavy duty partitioning for rear storage area New carpet throughout Photocopier, dyeline printer Signage on building façade designed by tenant	Custom-made furniture accommodates wiring in pedestal bases Task lighting throughout Internal p.a. system, telephones (dual system) New and purpose-made furnishing throughout Drawing files in garage, additional filing and storage in reproduction area at rear of space
General comments	
Sharp external image, convenient location near major motorway	Watchman patrols site (provided by complex)

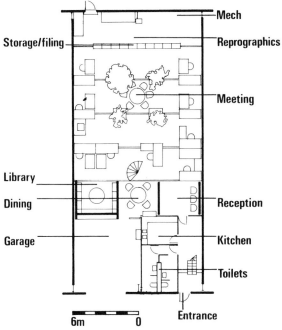

Storage/filing ── Mech
                  ── Reprographics

                  ── Meeting

Library ──
Dining ──   ── Reception

Garage ──   ── Kitchen

                  ── Toilets

6m   0   Entrance

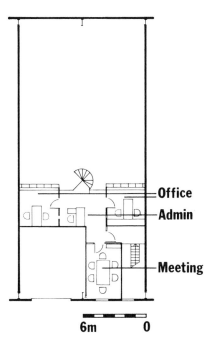

                  ── Office
                  ── Admin

                  ── Meeting

6m   0

Getting down to work with the minimum of adaptation

Firm H Date of occupation *c.* 1975	Design, manufacture and distribution of micro-processor based systems, including electronic pestal scales, data loggers and printers Employs 6 staff
Building prior to move-in (shell-related)	
New 'Advanced Factory Units' built by Milton Keynes Development Corporation, based on SBI system: steel frame with 12 × 12m bays Clear height 5.4m allows for two-storey offices. Cladding system of pressed metal plastic coated panels. Window openings and doors fit into modular cladding system Designed for both factory and office accommodation	Digitronix occupy approx 280m^2 lettable space. Water, gas, electricity distributed round perimeter. Natural ventilation. Gas hot air heating units. Electric water heater, fluorescent lighting suspended from roof structure Male and female toilets provided within unit
Building components and services after move-in (shell-related)	
Small workroom in production area constructed in blockwork	Electrical distribution expended. Security burglar-alarm system
Independent components and services after move-in (scenery-related)	
Steel structure erected independent of building shell, containing mezzanine floor and staircase for storage of product components	Fluorescent task lighting Knock down work bench system Office area carpeted Second-hand furniture
General comments	
Assembly of benching, store area by in-house staff	Minimum of work carried out to inhabit building shell

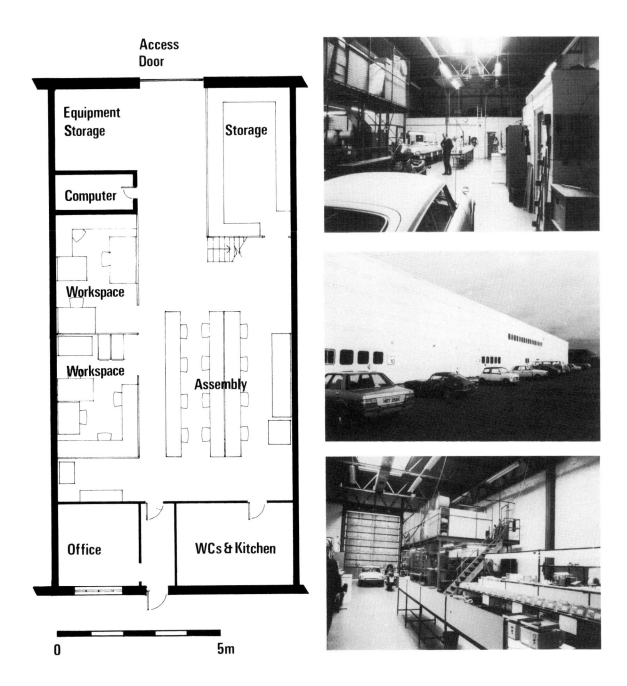

Access
Door

Equipment
Storage

Storage

Computer

Workspace

Workspace

Assembly

Office

WCs & Kitchen

0   5m

PART 3

Fitting-out Component Guide

Introduction

Traditional interiors were crafted out of basic materials and inseparable from the form of the building. Today's interiors are assembled from mass-produced, off-the-shelf components. Walls can be rapidly erected from pre-finished, pre-wired panels, ceilings formed from components with integrated lighting acoustics and extract, and floors rapidly finished with easily changeable carpet tiles. The final assemblage takes a fraction of the time of traditional on-site crafts with the minimum of upheaval.

The components for the workplace interior are supplied from a variety of sources: the traditional building industry (partitions, ceilings, lighting, etc); contract furniture manufacturers (storage, desks, etc); specialist equipment suppliers (packaged air-conditioning, waste disposal skips) contract interiors. This section draws from all these sources and provides an easily usable catalogue to the main suppliers of a comprehensive range of off-the-shelf components that may be required to adapt a raw shell for use as laboratory, showroom or office space, or for distribution. The selection ranges from the large elements for sub-division to ephemera such as nameplates and blinds.

The elements are organised according to whether they are fixed to or have an impact on the building shell and require traditional building contracting services – building components and services; and those elements which are provided by specialist suppliers or the contract furniture trades and are freestanding of the shell – internal scenery. **13 a, b** identifies the two categories of elements.

Building components and services (shell-related) are used to adapt the building shell, and are dependent on fixing, tolerances and the dimensional demands of more traditional building trades. This category includes:

Building components

— partitions
— suspended ceilings
— floors – raised access
— solar control – external

Building services

— power supply – trunking
— lighting
— fire protection
— plumbing – toilet and water supply
— water heating

— ventilation; air extraction
— ventilation; heating, cooling, air-conditioning
— heating

Internal scenery is installed independently within the building shell, and is supportive of specific activities. This category includes:

Independent components

— screens (heavy duty)
— screens (light duty)
— floor finishes
— mezzanine floors
— material handling: lifting equipment
— external elements

Independent services

— security
— communications systems

Furniture, fittings and accessories

— furniture: office systems
— office storage
— special furniture and fittings
— industrial and scientific systems fittings and storage
— solar control – internal
— signage

Information about each element is organised to provide:

— The percentage amount of the total fitting-out budget that might be spent on the element for office, laboratory or light industrial usage.
— A short description of specification and usage.
— Critical issues to be considered when specifying the element, including:
— flexibility
— construction
— method of fixing
— sound insulation
— fire resistance
— services
— finishes
— cost

The tables for each element show basic, medium and high levels of specification for each element and a corresponding list of manufacturers who supply the elements at that level of specification.

46

Figure 13.
a) Shell and service-related components that are fitted to the shell.
b) Independent and 'scenery' components that are installed independently of the building shell.

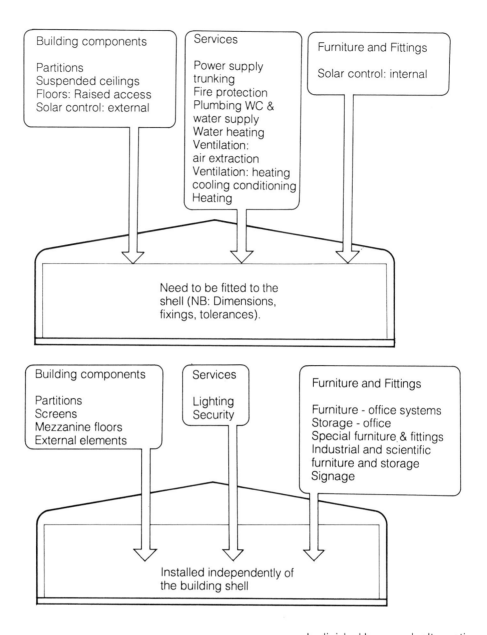

Costs

Table 11 (p.22) gives a cost per m² of gross floor area (GFA) for the basic, medium and high level of specification of each element. For a rough guide to cost:
— take each element and decide which specification you require;
— list the £/m² per GFA of each element (depending on whether office or industrial building) in Table 11;
— add together for total cost per m² of gross floor area.
By this method, the cost per m² can be adjusted very quickly by changing the levels of specification of various elements. See example in Table 12.

Sequence of Fitting-Out

Take an empty shell, **14a**. Decide how the shell and services may need to be adapted to meet the specific firm's demands, **14b**. External openings may be changed, solar control added, air-handling equipment installed, a raised floor considered to deal with computer wiring, and

spaces sub-divided by round, alternating partitioning. Finally, each space will require a furniture, fittings and accessories check to adjust the space to specific activities, **14c**. The quality and budget cost of each element chosen will depend on the usages (office, industrial) to be accommodated (Section II).

Figure 14.
a) Typical empty shell.
b) Shell with services and building components added to adjust to the firm's functions.
c) Movable furniture and equipment for specific activities.

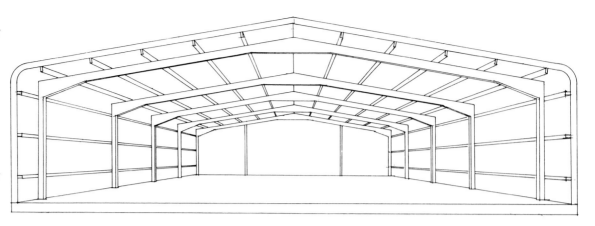

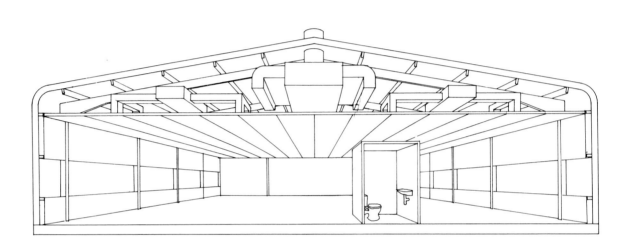

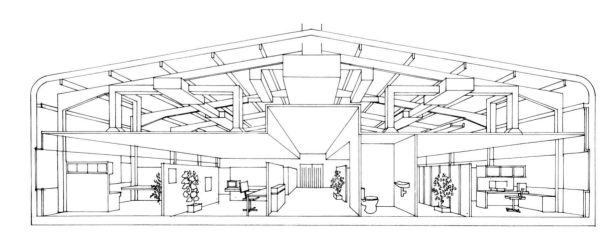

BUILDING COMPONENTS

Internal sub-division – partitions

Lightweight, non-loadbearing divisions between spaces to form secure and soundproof enclosures. (See also Screens, p.80.) Partitioning of one or another kind is a major element in any office layout and can have many functions other than security and sound reduction. It can, for example, assist work flow and privacy, eliminate distraction and act as a boundary or barrier. Demountable partitions, while offering the easiest method of adapting an office to changing requirements, are expensive. A good quality metal framed system will cost 2–3 times as much as a plastered masonry partition. To help decide on the system and level of specification required the following must be considered/determined.

Flexibility/demountability

— What degree of flexibility will be required? How often are divisions between spaces likely to be changed? If only at intervals of several years, flexibility is not a major factor.

— The advantage of increased future flexibility must be weighed against probable extra cost and possible reduction in sound insulation. The flexibility of the services provision/installation must be considered.

— If flexibility is of prime importance full-height partitions may not be an ideal solution; an alternative is open-plan space with freestanding screens (see p.80).

Construction

— The degree of dimensional tolerance required will influence the basic type of system selected, i.e. loose fit (site assembled with adjustable dimensions; particularly suitable for adapting old buildings) or tight fit (factory assembled and modular). The basic construction types (excluding masonry) are:

● Stud/sheet systems (loose fit): timber or steel study covered with sheet material; both can be cut to size on site. Not easily demountable.
● Frame/sheet systems (relatively loose fit): exposed framework (metal or wood) at fairly wide intervals, with vertical and horizontal studs between, covered with sheet material; components can, where required, usually be cut to size on site.
● Frame/panel systems (tight fit): frame and panel delivered to site ready assembled and units joined together to form partition.
● Panel/panel systems (tight fit): factory finished self-supporting panels, butt jointed and fixed top and bottom to form partition.

— Method of fixing must be investigated. Adjoining surfaces (walls, floors, ceilings) must not be damaged. Consider inter-relationship between the module of partitioning system and that of suspended ceiling system.

— Are partitions required to support shelves, storage units, etc? Not all systems make provision for this. If storage is required as an integral part of the partitioning, see Storage: offices, on p.101.

Sound insulation

— Information given by manufacturers can be misleading if for panel only. In situ leakage of sound can occur through doors, glazed areas and joints between partitions and other elements.

— The average solid full height partition will give a sound reduction level of around 30dB, which is satisfactory for spaces in which background noise is acceptable. Certain rooms (e.g. directors' offices, libraries, etc) will require reduction of around 45db.

Fire resistance

— Building Regulations and requirements of Fire Authorities in respect of combustability and the rate of spread of flame will affect the choice of system. A notional period of fire resistance for ½–1 hour will be adequate for most situations.

Services

— Does design of shell make provision for services in perimeter trunking, vertical ducts, ceilings, access floors, etc? Services built into partitioning will limit the degree of flexibility.

Finishes

— Panels can be obtained in a variety of finishes, e.g. paint, plastic laminates, hessian, vinyl and hardwood veneers. Suitability of various finishes will be determined by considering individual requirements with regard to appearance and character; impact resistance; maintenance and cleaning; sound absorption; treatment of adjoining surfaces; cost.

— Frames may be of aluminium (usually anodised), steel (painted or stove enamelled) or hardwood.

Glazing

— Will glazing be required for any of the following reasons: borrowed light for corridor or other space; supervisory purposes; aesthetic reasons, e.g. decoration or sense of spaciousness?

— Glazing can affect sound insulation (double glazing should be used), and incorporation of services.

Cost

Compare the installation, maintenance and in-use costs for the systems under consideration.

Table 14 Partitions. Levels of specification and manufacturers.

Basic level of specification	Suppliers and manufacturers	
Masonry (largely permanent party walls, solid or glazed): of bricks, blocks or storey-height panels. This type of division between spaces is not easily demountable and is a wet construction method but can have certain advantages, e.g. good sound reduction and fire resistance, ability to support fittings and relatively low cost.	Aerated Concrete	Siporex
	ARC Concrete	Conbloc
	Beachcroft	D2S
	Celcon	Celcon
	Plasmor	Stanlite
	Tarmac Pellite	Pellite
	Thermalite	Thermalite
Bricks: most expensive take longest to erect.		
Blocks: usually concrete; available in wide range (solid, cellular and hollow) with differing densities and characteristics for various applications.		
Panels: various proprietary types available.		
Stud and sheet systems: sheets of plasterboard 'egg-box' construction, compressed straw or woodwool slabs, chipboard, or metal secured to and supported by concealed timber or metal studs.	Anderson Construction	Firecoust
	British Gypsum	Paramount Dry Partition
	Clifford	Sonic-fire partitioning
	Deewall Contracts	Metal Stud Partitions
	Holland, Hannon & Cubitts	Cubitt/Neslo Flushwall
	Movable Drywall	Cor-met (frame/sheet system – can be made demountable)
	Scandia Steel	Isolamin 32B and 40c (simple panel-to-panel systems)
	Stramit Systems	Plaslin and Drylin
	Welconstruct	1200 SF
Medium level of specification		
Non-fire resistant demountable systems. Lightweight, dry construction but sound reduction level may be low, i.e. 25–30dB.	Apton	Budget Q Line
	Cashman Erectors	Paragon
	Conder Group	Conder system
	Deewall Contracts	Aluminium framed partitioning
	EPS	Eiderline
	Firmin & Collins	Flushform
	Flexi-plan	Executive
	Hatmet Contracts	Permalock systems
	Howick	SP Executive A and ASE
	Key Industrial	Keytex
	Killby & Gayford	Kaygee Flush, PA and Slimline
	Petra Partitions	System 1
	Robseal	600 Series
	Roneo Vickers	System 70
	Spacenay Design	Executive
	Unilock Partitions	Slenderdee
	Versitile Fittings	Versi-wall
	Welconstruct	1200 C
Fire resistant tight fit systems which are easily demountable, lightweight and of dry construction. Fittings and accessories not an integral part of system. Materials of frames and panels, and finishes vary depending on requirements and on system. Sound reduction good and fire resistance half-hour upwards.	Anderson Construction	Firestud and aluminium framed systems
	Apton	Budget Q Line and Maars
	Burntwood	Pyro 39 system
	Cape Durasteel	Durasteel Fire Partitions
	Cashman Erectors	Paragon 30 and 60
	Clifford	Aluminium framed partitioning
	Compactom	Tenon fire
	Firmin & Collins	PMS Mark 4

	Flexi-plan	Sound fire 1
	GTE Unistrut	Partition systems
	Hatmet Contractors	Permalock Standard
	Holland Hannon & Cubitt	Cubitt/Neslo Firewall
	Howick	AS and AS2
	Interfinish Partitions	Finish 7OAL and 100DM
	Internal British Systems	Inter Plan system with Fire Plan panels
	L & D Installations	Master range
	Moveable Drywall	Coreform and Corelock
	Norwood	President 2 and 3 and Firebreak
	OAST	Harmony systems
	Paxwood	Conderscreen 900
	Phoenix Roll-formed Sections	Safe 'n Sound
	Robseal	600 Series
	Roneo Vickers	System 100 and 2LF
	Roskel	Aluminium framed systems
	Service Partitions	SP systems
	Unilock-Curtis Steel	Concorde
	Unilock Partitions	Firesound
	Unistrut	Warwick systems
	United Storage	Excelsior range
	Voko	Range of partitions
	Vosseler	VF Range

High level of specification

Non-fire resistant movable/instantly demountable partitions. Sliding, sliding/folding with ceiling track, or removable panels locked against floor and ceiling. Sound reduction level may be low. For use in areas where flexibility is vital, e.g. room dividers.	Acordial	Plancord and Ferrowall (movable suspended), and Acordial and Lignacord (sliding folding)
	British Fairwall	Airwall and Atlas (removable), and Kett folding
	Hewetson	Modernfold and Divisiflex
	Marley	Marleyfold
	Project Interiors	Multiflex and Variflex
	SMP	Lockwall, Track Lockwall and LW 100
	WHN National Products	Pella (wood folding)
Fire resistant movable/instantly demountable partitions. As above but usually metal panels either suspended from track or held rigid by pressure to floor and ceiling. Sound reduction better than above and fire resistance of half hour. For use in areas where high flexibility is vital, e.g. room dividers.	Acordial	FerrowallFS and Planacord Super
	British Fairwall	Atlas and Kett
	SMP	Lockwall, Track Lockwall and LW 100
As under 'medium' specification but of increased level, i.e. sound reduction; fire resistance; range of accessories and storage units forming integral part of system (ability to form wall of storage and/or work surface). For storage walls see 'High' specification on page 103.	Arrange Marketing	Holzapfel and Interwand
	Flexi-plan	Soundfire 2
	Hauserman	Accord, Ambiance and Hauserman/Steelcase systems
	Howick	AS2 Executive
	LM Partitions	Design 2000 system
	Mason Nordia	Nordia
	Medfurn Interiors	Deko
	Unilock Partitions	Context Safewall
	Voko	Partitioning and wall units

Suspended ceilings

Ceiling hung at a distance from wall or roof above and not bearing on the walls. The space between ceiling and main structure (slab or roof) over is usually used for services – heating, lighting, ventilation, etc.

Suspended ceilings may be composed of three basic elements: the suspension (or fixing) system; the sheet, panel or tile surface; and service units such as lights, air-conditioning diffusers and sprinklers. There is a wide variety of proprietary systems, some of which are fully integrated and consist of all three elements. Before deciding on a system and level of specification the following must be considered/ determined.

Basic requirements

— To what extent must the ceiling be sound absorbent? This will affect the choice of system and the type of material used for the infill panels, some of which are textured or perforated (sometimes with a sound absorbent blanket laid over the top) to increase the absorbency.
— Is it important that the ceiling should contribute to the thermal resistance (reduction of heat loss and solar gain) of the roof? A thermally efficient ceiling could be a necessity under a typical industrial roof construction or in cases where a heat recovery system is to be used.
— To what extent must services – lighting, ventilation, air-conditioning, heating, etc – be integrated with the ceiling? This will affect the choice of system, e.g. where a high degree of integration is required a jointless ceiling will be unsuitable.

Ceiling types

— When priorities have been established consider which basic type may be most suitable:

● Jointless: lath and plaster or plasterboard suspended on timber or metal framework.
● Frame (or grid) and panel/tile: suspended grid, usually of metal sections, with infill of fibreboard of mineral fibre tiles, metal trays, three- dimensional panels, etc. The grid system can be exposed, concealed or semi-exposed.
● Linear strip: suspended supports in one direction only, carrying ceiling strips (usually of metal) which can be open faced – fixed with space between the strips – or closed faced.
● Illuminated: either louvres, open grid panels or translucent panels. The light source in this system is in the space between ceiling and main structure. In other systems light fittings either fit into ceiling grid or are fixed below.

Access

— What degree of access to the void behind the ceiling is required? It must be possible to reach all the service pipes, cables and fittings; the more heavily serviced the space, the more access will be required.
— A few pre-determined access points can be provided in all systems. Exposed grid frames with removable modular panels provide the easiest way of obtaining access throughout.

Fire resistance

— Building regulations and requirements of Fire Authorities will affect choice; jointless ceilings will usually be the most resistant while the open grid type will be least effective.
— The void above the ceiling can act as a horizontal flue and carry smoke, gases and sparks from one part of the office to another. Vertical fire stop baffles may be required.

Weight and strength

— Consider the weight of the suspended ceiling as it must be supported by the main structure. Jointless ceilings are heaviest weighing between 20 and 50 kg/m^2; frame and panel normally weigh between 5 and 15 kg/m^2 and linear strip between 3 and 5 kg/m^2.
— Can the ceiling support the required light fittings and other service elements?

General considerations

— If sound insulation between spaces is of prime importance partitions may have to be carried up to the underside of the structural floor to prevent sound passing over the top of partitions through the suspended ceiling. Consider how this will affect the flexibility of the space; also the inter-relationship between the modules of the ceiling and partitioning systems.
— Consider the thermal conductivity (k value) for the different materials and different thicknesses of each material.
— Will ceiling ventilation be required, e.g. in computer rooms? Perforated steel trays are widely accepted as the most suitable solution.

Finishes

— Consider the overall effect required. The various types of ceilings and the various finishes available will differ greatly in appearance.
— When assessing alternatives, consider how much maintenance will be required and how easily the ceiling can be cleaned.

Cost

— Compare the installation, maintenance and in-use costs for the systems under consideration.
— The more fully integrated the ceiling the more expensive it will be. It may, however, help to provide increased flexibility in the use of the space below.

Table 15 Suspended ceilings. Levels of specification and manufacturers.

Basic level of specification	Suppliers and manufacturers	
Jointless and often non-proprietary, e.g. plaster on metal lathing plasterboard, stretched sheet plastic membrane, etc. This type of ceiling is not easily demountable nor does it have flexibility in terms of access.	British Gypsum Environaire	Gyproc Spanoflex
Simple frame and panel or plank ceilings or linings. Service concealment, sound absorption and thermal insulation are provided at relatively low cost. Trunking, to which light fittings are attached, may be included as an integral part of the ceiling.	Cape Boards Celotex Donn Products Fibreglass Merchant Trading	Supalux ceiling panels and planks Lining Grid System Donn Liner system Factory liner Metco MF4
Medium level of specification		
Modular frame and panel or linear strip sound absorbent ceilings with easy access. Grid may be: exposed – provides greatest flexibility at lowest cost; concealed – more sophisticated and complicated, and more expensive to install.	Anderson Construction Armstrong Cork Burgess Celotex Donn Products Hunter Douglas Fairline Interlite Linear Rowledge Trectex Acoustic	Aluphon range Trulock grid with Ceramaguard or various other panels Various, e.g. Standard tile, Modulam and Caprilux Acousti-Grid with various panel materials Paraline and DP Pan Grid ceiling system Luxalon range System 100 and Xtra Span Interlux-Interclip Ritone Trectex grids with various panel
Louvre/open grid ceiling of metal, plastic or wood with lighting and other services usually mounted on main structure above ceiling. Access and demountability easy but performance poor in terms of sound absorption/reduction and fire resistance.	Anderson Construction Burgess Dampa Formwood Hunter Douglas	Aluphon Spaljett and Baffles Ecranlux Dampa Baffle System Formalux 125 & 60 Mallite Luxalon V100 and V200 also grid type
High level of specification		
Flat or moulded sound absorbent ceilings with high degree of services integration, including coffered or shaped panels which may contain light fittings.	Armstrong Cork Burgess Dampa Hauserman	Luminaire Metalflair Dampa-Tiles Compac Regular and
Ventilated, dust-free, sound absorbent ceilings suitable for special areas (e.g. computer rooms). Usually of perforated metal panels which can function as an air-handling membrane. Part of the area covered with sound absorbent pads enclosed in plastic envelopes to give lint-free conditions. By altering position of free openings the air distribution pattern can easily be corrected or adjusted.	Burgess Dampa Flairline Hauserman	Standard Tiles, Longspan Panels Dampa-10 Type P System 100 and Extra Span Compac

Floors: raised access

Self-supporting floor over the structural sub-floor forming an accessible void in which services can be run for flexible provision of outlets for lights, power, computer terminals, telephones, etc. (See also Power supply: trunking, p.57.)
The use of raised access floors should be considered for computer rooms and other heavily serviced areas. Before deciding on a system and level of specification the following should be considered/determined:

Basic considerations

— Is a floor void space with access the best solution or could trunking provide the required degree of servicing and flexibility? See p.57.
— Determine exactly what is to be run in the floor space and at what intervals surface connections will be required. This will influence the depth of void needed and the number of access points to the void, e.g. every panel removable or access at pre-determined points only.
— Is underfloor void to be used as plenium for air-conditioning/ventilation? Special perforated panels or air grilles may be required.

Types

— There are two basic types of access floor:

• Shallow (cavity less than 100 mm high): these are usually of timber construction with a limited number of access panels. The shallow void space will only accommodate electrical and telephone cables.
• Deep (cavity more than 100 mm high): supports are normally of steel with adjustable pedestals and access is possible over the whole area. The void may be used for not only cables and pipes but also air-conditioning.

Loading and construction

— Is the surface of the sub-floor in good condition and relatively level? Make sure that the levelling mechanism of the access floor is capable of taking up the necessary tolerance.
— Must floor be suitable for heavy duty use? If

heavy equipment and machinery will be used or stand on floor a suitable system must be selected, i.e. supports must be adequate; panel size will also be affected.
— Make certain that the support and panel system will be rigid when assembled; vibration and resonance must be reduced to a minimum. Most systems allow for stringers (horizontal bearers) to be added for additional support and rigidity if required.
— Building Regulations and requirements of Fire Authorities may affect choice of system. Some systems have panels formed from metal incorporating an insulated core to ensure maximum fire resistance.

General considerations

— How much flexibility do the systems under consideration have? Can power points and telephone outlets be easily and quickly relocated without specialist assistance?
— Is the system to be used in a computer room? If so, will it provide acceptable electrical resistance if anti-static PVC or carpet is to be fitted?

Finish

— In some cases choice of finish may be limited to those which can be laid on a timber base.
— The most common finishes are carpeting, PVC, linoleum and plastic laminate. In computer rooms floor finish must be anti-static.
— Suitability of finish will be determined by considering individual requirements with regard to appearance; cleaning and maintenance; durability, etc. (See also Floors: finishes, p.84.)

Cost

— Compare the installation, maintenance and in use costs for the systems under consideration.

Table 16 Floors, raised access. Levels of specification and manufacturers.

Medium level of specification	Suppliers and manufacturers	
Shallow floor with limited access – removable panels usually fitted where required. Deck material commonly of chipboard and supports may be of timber and non-adjustable. Fire resistance and loading capacity may be low.	Contiwood	Lombard
	Corewind	Ductaflor
	Donn Products	Raised floor system with mini-pedestals
	Hewetson	Lodeck
	Propaflor	Spacedeck and Guardian Office Load
	Robertson	Buroplan 300 and Platform Floor-Partial Access System
	System Floors	System 300
High level of specification		
Deep floor with high degree of accessibility. Adjustable supports of steel and deck of steel or chipboard with sheet steel backing. Fire resistance and loading capacity generally relatively high.	Corewind	Computaflor
	Denco Miller	Raised modular floors
	Dorm Products	Raised modular floors
	Hewetson	Tate S800 Series, Ram C600 and Adder G600
	Hiross	Access floor systems
	Hoechst	Goldback raised floors
	Intek	Raised modular floors
	Metacoustic	MK20 system
	Project Interiors	Datafloor and Confordalle
	Promotional World	Mero
	Propaflor	Guardian and Propadek ranges
	Robertson	Platform Floor and Cavity Floor ranges
	Systems Floors	System 1260, 1200 and 600
	Unistrut	Raised floor system

Solar control: external

Devices to protect openings – particularly windows – from direct solar radiation and rain, and to reduce or control sky glare.
External shading or screening is the most effective way of protecting windows from solar radiation, and thus of eliminating or reducing summer heat gain from this source. To decide on the appropriate method and level of specification the following must be considered/determined:

Basic requirements

— Will it be possible to use some form of external shading device, e.g. if premises is in part of an existing building? If not, it may be necessary to consider an alternative method (see p.112.)
— What sizes are the openings that need protection and what is their orientation? Different forms of shading will be required, depending on the orientation, and the height of a window will, for example, affect the distance a horizontal canopy must project out from the face of the wall.
— Must the screening do more than simply provide protection from solar radiation? For example, temporary control or exclusion of

daylight or to give privacy at times.

Calculations

— Specialist help will be required to calculate shading requirements and to check the efficiency of the proposed screening for the various orientations, for any time of the day, any day of the year.
— The period when shading will be needed must be determined (from average temperatures for different times of the year and different times of the day), i.e. it is usually necessary to exclude sun during the summer but admit it during the cooler periods.
— The position of the sun, during the period when shading is needed, will have to be determined by using a special sun-path diagram. A protractor, having the same scale as the sun-path diagram, can then be used to determine the type and position of the shading device.
— Shading devices produce what are called 'shading masks' – these represent the section of the sky which they will obscure – which can be simply resolved into one of three basic types: vertical, where the characteristic shape is bounded by radial lines; horizontal, with a mask of segmental shape; and egg-crate types, which

are a combination of the first two.

Methods

— In many cases, different shading devices will leave similar masks, so that several possible solutions to a shading problem will usually exist.

— The following are the main types of standard shading devices:

• External Venetian blinds with slats of aluminium or stainless steel. They are adjustable from inside the building.
• Vertical and horizontal fins and louvres, either fixed or adjustable. May be of metal, asbestos-cement, etc.
• Vertical screens which may consist of very small fixed louvres, mesh, egg-crate grill, perforated metal, etc.
• Horizontal canopies which may be of either solid or open (e.g. egg-crate or louvre) construction.
• Awnings; most commonly retractable with aluminium framework and fabric covering.

— The devices under consideration must be evaluated; their effectiveness depends upon how well they shade the glass in summer without shading it in winter and how well they perform the other functions expected of them, e.g. provide daylight control and/or privacy, etc.

General considerations

— A fixed device is not necessarily the best solution as the middle of summer does not necessarily coincide with the longest day of the year (21 June). Adjustable devices, however, are more expensive and require more maintenance. To be effective they need to be correctly adjusted.

— Canopies and other horizontal devices will not provide adequate protection for east and west facing windows and some form of vertical screen or a retractable blind will be required.

Operation and construction

— What type of operation is required for adjustable type devices – manual or electric, singly or in groups? Automatic solar control is also offered by some manufacturers.

— Do adjustable devices under consideration operate quietly and smoothly?

— Will the construction and the materials used be able to withstand normal wear and tear? How weatherproof are the materials and details?

— Will the device be able to withstand strong winds?

Appearance and maintenance

— Consider overall appearance in terms of effect required and compatibility with exterior elevation(s).

— Can moving parts, surfaces and fabrics be easily cleaned and maintained? How durable will they be?

Cost

— Compare the installation, maintenance and in-use costs for the systems under consideration.

Table 17 Solar control, external. Levels of specification and manufacturers.

Basic level of specification	Suppliers and manufacturers	
Horizontal canopies of solid or open construction; not adjustable.	Colt	Solar Screen
	Hunter Douglas	Luxalon 84R(E)
Retractable awnings; aluminium framework with fabric covering.	Amey Doors & Blinds	Range of awning and blinds
	J. Avery & Co.	Range of awnings
	Deans Blinds	Tropex and Continental
	Guildford Shares	Range of awnings
	Norman Hart	Range of awnings
	Perma Blinds	Range of awnings
	Solar Protection Equipment	Awning and blind systems
	Tidmarsh & Sons	Range of awnings and blinds
Medium level of specification		
Fixed solar control screens of metal louvres, grills, etc, in metal frame.	Colt	Kool Shade
Fixed vertical or horizontal fins or louvres.	Colt	Solar Screen
High level of specification		
Exterior Venetian blinds; adjustable with manual, electric or automatic operation.	J. Avery & Co. Bestobell	Reflex and VR90 Sunway external Venetian blinds

	Colt	Hippe ESC80 and 2000
	Faber	Maximatic external Venetian blinds
	Norman Hart	Maximatic external Venetian blinds
	Hunter Douglas	Luxaflex2 outside Venetian blinds
	Technical Blinds	T80
Adjustable, vertical or horizontal fins or louvres with manual, electric or automatic operation.	J. Avery & Co.	Edak Sunbreaker Fins (vertical or horizontal)
	Colt	Motorised fins and louvres
	Technical Blinds	Sunshield range (vertical or horizontal louvres)

BUILDING SERVICES

Power supply: trunking

Flexible electrical service systems (may also include telecommunications, data processing and alarm installations) which allow outlets to be added or subtracted easily at any time. (See also Floors: raised access, p.54.)

With the increased use of computers, VDUs and other electrically operated office equipment it is important to provide sufficient outlets of different types in convenient positions. The system may, furthermore, need to allow for easy access in the centre of the space and provide for flexibility of layout. Before deciding on a system and level of specification the following should be considered/determined:

Need

— What degree of flexibility/adaptability will be required? Will the positions and functions of spaces, and/or workstations within the space, need to be changed at fairly regular intervals?

— If maximum flexibility is a priority or a high degree of servicing is to be included in certain spaces, the use of some form of trunking will be justified.

System

— The size and type of space (e.g. office, laboratory, etc), the type and position of equipment to be provided for, the degree of servicing required, and the degree of flexibility/adaptability needed, will all influence the choice of basic system.

● Floor or ceiling trunking, possibly in combination with vertical power poles, may be used where workstations must be placed well away from walls. In certain situations overhead distribution may be more economical and more flexible than floor systems.

● Perimeter wall trunking (skirting or dado) may be useful in offices, laboratories, etc, where workstations are close to or against walls.

● Special trunking (e.g. bench trunking, overhead booms, etc) may be most suitable in specialised areas such as laboratories, assembly areas and workshops.

Detail considerations

— The size and type of trunking channel will be determined by the various services which must be run in it. It is essential that the services contained in the channel are partitioned from each other.

— How simple is the system? Can tap-off units be added and moved easily without specialist assistance?

— How robust is the system? Will it stand up to the wear and tear of continual handling and alteration? Some are made of metal, others of extruded uPVC (unplasticised polyvinyl chloride).

— Consider the appearance of the system – the channel, cover strips, fittings, finishes, etc.

— If skirting trunking is being considered, are threshold units available? This must be considered if trunking will be on a wall which may contain doors.

Flexibility

— Can channels be cut easily and taken around corners, columns, etc?

— Can the system be removed and re-used elsewhere? This will not be the case with those forming an integral part of either the floor or the ceiling.

— Is there a wide range of accessories available as an integral part of the system?

— Ensure that the system can be designed so that trunking cover strips can always be easily removed to reach cables, e.g. skirting trunking on external walls must allow for cover to be removed between demountable partitioning in various positions.

Cost

— Compare the installation, maintenance and in-use costs for the systems under consideration.

Table 18 Power supply; trunking. Levels of specification and manufacturers.

Basic level of specification	Suppliers and manufacturers	
Flexible extension leads plugged into sockets at fixed positions on ceiling track. One double outlet per 20 m².	Ackermann BICC	Hanging service module Curliflex with sockets suitable for fixing to trunking, e.g. Wandsworth Comet 13 amp shallow depth socket
	Egatube	Masterflex
Simple perimeter or ceiling trunking (one or two compartments) for wiring with integral accessory boxes in fixed position. Suitable for re-wiring converted older properties.	Barton Cableduct Davis Egatube Gilflex-Key Legrand RADA & SLR	Standard cable trunking CD Standard Surface Trunking Type C Davex lastic trunking Ega Compact Miniature Trunking Mini-trunking and Mini Service Trunking for Carpets Mini-trunking ES15 and Onward services trunking

Medium level of specification (see also Floors: raised access)

Continuous ceiling track with power tap-off from any position (or regularly spaced positions) on track. Some of the track/tubular lighting systems make provisions for power cables, etc. See high level of specification p.59, and Floors: raised access.	Barton Cableduct Davis Egatube Electrak Erco Klockner-Moeller Martingale Philips Simplex Thorsman Unirax	Buslight lighting trunking CD Lighting Trunking Clipped Trunking Norwich Trunking Electrak system 1-circuit and 3-circuit tracks with accessories CD-System Integrated Ceiling Services Litebeam Trunking Systems Vistalite, Hi-duct and Versaduct Inka Ceiling System Unirax Standard Trunking
Skirting trunking with at least two compartments with removable covers. With tap-off from any position (or regularly spaced positions) for power and telephones; also with range of integral fittings and accessories. May be combined with floor system.	Achermann Barton Cableduct Davis Egatube Electrak Gilflex-Key Legrand Martingale Unirax	Service rail and perimeter trunking Standard surface pattern skirting trunking CD skirting trunking Skirting trunking Lincoln Skirting System and Liverpool Electrak System System 3500 Skirting trunking Extruded Aluminium Trunking Bevelled and Square skirting trunking
Underfloor trunking comprising a wiring duct with concealed, flush or pedestal outlets and a range of integral accessories. May be combined with skirting trunking and power poles.	Ackermann Barton Cableduct Davis	Flush floor trunking system Flush floor trunking system CD Underfloor and CD Flush Floor trunking Floor trunking systems

Gilflex-Key	System 3100 and System 3200
Unirax	Underfloor and Flush Floor trunking

High level of specification (see also Floors: raised access)

Vertical rigid service poles with adjustable jack to allow for variations in ceiling heights. With compartments for electrical power, telephones, data circuits, etc, and range of integral fittings and accessories. Combined with ceiling or floor distribution system.

Dado or bench trunking for special applications and those with diverse and complex service requirements. With at least two, and usually three compartments (each with separate cover in some cases), and a range of integral fittings and accessories. Some systems include a separate electronic cable duct to ensure complete screening of computer/VDU cable.

High level of specification

Ackermann	ISS80 service pole
Cableduct	CD Service Pole
Davis	Trimline Column and Slimline Column
Gilflex-Key	Delta Service Pole
Ackermann	Technodrant desk unit
Barton	Bench trunking
Cableduct	CD Dado Trunking
David	Bench trunking
Eggtube	Sealand and Glasgow bench trunking
Electrak	Electrak system
Gilflex-Key	TC 152 dado trunking
Legrand	Above-skirting trunking
Sintacel	Overhead Service System
Unirax	Bench trunking

Lighting

Artificial lighting either to supplement natural daylight and for after dark use, or to provide a totally artificially lit interior.
The determination of the correct lighting conditions for different environments is a complicated task and is affected by a variety of factors; specialist advice must be obtained. To help decide on the type of lighting and the level of specification the following must be considered/determined:

Basic strategy

— Consider what visual tasks must be provided for. Consider the shapes of the spaces in relation to the sizes and positions of windows.
— Will natural lighting be possible or practical? The depth to which it can penetrate is limited. Also, the size, position and design of glazed areas will be affected by various factors in addition to the level of lighting required, e.g. view, privacy, glare, noise, etc.
— Which of the following will be most appropriate? Daylight only with artificial light for use at night and when daylight level is inadequate; daylight permanently supplemented by artificial light; artificial lighting only?
— Consider energy conservation – remember, however, that a number of factors are involved. For example, windows can in themselves be energy inefficient (allowing heat loss in winter and solar gain in summer) if not correctly designed.

Level of illuminance

— In the type of spaces under consideration it is often difficult to provide suitable working conditions with daylight alone: carefully integrated artificial lighting will almost certainly be needed.
— What amount of lighting will be required in each of the spaces? Illuminance – the amount of light falling on to a surface – is measured in lux (lumens/m^2) and the level will depend on the type of task being performed, i.e. the more detailed and exacting, the higher the illuminance.
— The following list gives a general guide to the illuminance required on working level:

Executive and general offices	500 lux
Typing and business machines	750 lux
Filing rooms	300 lux
Computer rooms	500 lux
Drawing offices	500 lux (general); 750 lux (on drawing board)
Industrial assembly areas	500 lux (medium work) 1000 lux (fine work, e.g. electronic assembly); 1500 lux (very fine work)
Laboratories	500–700 lux
Storage and circulation areas	150 lux (at floor level)

Quality of light

— Not only must task lighting level be correct but pleasant general lighting conditions must also be created. Consider following factors:

• Glare; which can have a disabling effect or cause discomfort.
• Relative brightness of surrounding surfaces which is affected by their reflection, colour, etc.
• Colour rendering of objects seen under the light source, i.e. compared with that under daylight conditions.
• Colour appearance, i.e. colour of the light source; usually expressed as being warm, intermediate or cool.
• Directional characteristics of the light.
• Veiling reflections (bright reflections in the task): particular care must be taken with visual display unit screens. Indirect illumination systems (e.g. uplighters) usually give good conditions.

Lamps and luminaires

— Once the required illuminance and lighting quality have been determined, suitable types of lamps and luminaires can be selected.
— Lamps divide into three main categories:

• Filament (warm appearance): these have short lives and high running costs. Often used for supplementary lighting but seldom as main (or general) source. Tungsten-halogen more efficient than conventional types.
• Tubular fluorescent (generally intermediate but warm and cool also available). Most used lamp type in offices, laboratories, etc. Main advantages: low brightness, long life, high efficiency and wide range of sizes and colours. Flicker may be a problem.
• High pressure discharge lamps: various types available, e.g. colour corrected mercury lamps (colour appearance and rendering similar to daylight fluorescent); mercury halide lamps – take a long time to warm up and if switched off take ten minutes to relight; high pressure sodium – golden yellow light widely used in industry.

— Luminaires have various functions – supply current, support lamps, dissipate heat, etc – but main role is to control distribution of light from lamps. Another important feature is method of mounting, e.g. recessed, semi-recessed, pendant, bracket, etc.
— Light control may be by obstruction (opaque enclosures with direct or indirect lighting), diffusion (enclosing lamp in translucent shade), reflection, and refraction (shade of glass or plastic prism material). Luminaires often combine methods; reflectors above lamps, for example, with diffusers or prismatic controllers below. Uplighters – which beam light on to the ceiling from where it is cast down multidirectionally – are being increasingly used; height of luminaire is important, i.e. at least 1.7 m above eye level.

Lighting systems

— Once the appropriate lamp/luminaire combinations have been chosen the system –

including location and arrangement of lighting – must be settled. Decisions taken at this stage may require revision of earlier choices, i.e. lamps and luminaires. Consider the following basic systems:

• General lighting: more or less regular arrangement of luminaires over ceiling area to give uniform illuminance in space. Disadvantage: waste of energy in large spaces as areas not used for work are lit to unnecessarily high level. Advantage: flexibility of positions for workstations.
• Directional lighting: shines from preferred direction and is often used for display lighting; may also be combined with general lighting.
• Localised lighting: generally ceiling mounted – predetermined areas lit to required task level while other areas have less light. Satisfactory if positions of workstations are fixed.
• Local lighting: used to supplement a separate system of general lighting with luminaires provided close to task, illuminating only a small area. Can be extremely flexible if well designed. This form of lighting is integrated into some furniture systems (see p.100).

Control (of lighting and heat)

— Consider how the various forms of lighting can be most effectively controlled to give maximum flexibility. Rows of luminaires on separate switches; individual switching for task lighting; manually operated switches and/or automatic controls for general lighting, etc. Automatic controls vary from sample time clocks to complex daylight season systems.
— What lighting will be used for cleaning, security and safety? How will it be controlled?
— Artificial lighting can create problems of overheating of spaces during summer. Special air-handling luminaires, together with an appropriate ventilation/heat recovery system (or air-conditioning), provide a solution.

Maintenance and cleaning

— How easy will it be to clean and maintain the different types of luminaires under consideration? Accessibility is important. Can fitting be easily removed for servicing or replacement.

Cost

— Compare the installation, maintenance and in-use costs for the systems being considered.
— Although the initial costs of filament lamps and fittings are lower than for fluorescent, running costs are higher when the installation is in regular use for long periods. More electricity is required for a given level of illumination and lamp replacement is more frequent.
— Consider tax advantage of task/local lighting (e.g. freestanding, desk mounted, etc) becoming a movable asset.

Table 19 Lighting. Levels of specification and manufacturers.

Basic level of specification (500 lux at workplace)	Suppliers and manufacturers	
General or localised lighting using luminaires (1/19 m²) with two 1.80 m fluorescent tubes and opal diffusers or prismatic controllers. Mounted on ceiling or ceiling track. (See also Trunking, p.57.)	AEG-Telefunken	Multilux A and Galaxielux ranges; also Gealux pre-wired trunking with plug-in luminaires
	Ascog	Various ranges of surface luminaires
	Barton	Buslight trunking and pre-wired industrial lighting trunking
	BBI Lighting	Visolite range and trunking with fittings
	Courtney Pope	Topmost and other ranges
	Crompton Parkinson	Crompack and other ranges
	Erco	Uminair and Vision ranges
	IMS Lighting	Prestilum
	LDMS	Fagerhults 1200 Series and other ranges
	Lumitron	Diplomat, National and other ranges
	Marlin	Prismax range
	Moorlite	Target, Classic and other ranges; also Compete 2 trunking
	Osram	Speedpack range
	Philips	Streamlite, Popular and other ranges; also Featureline prewired trunking with plug-in luminaires
	Raak	Basic light range
	RADA & SLR	Surface Module range; also lighting and trunking system
	Simplex	FAL and Tilite pre-wired trunking
	Spectrum	Herbst range
	Thorn Lighting	Clipper trunking and luminaires, and other ranges
	Unirax	lighting trunking
	Unistrut	lighting trunking
Industrial type lighting	AEG-Telefunken	Megalux Low Bay
	Iris Lighting	Pyralum and RC industrial fittings
	Philips	Hermes 2
	Thorn Lighting	Hipack Industrial, Lopack Compact and Invincible fittings
	Victor Products	Regent range of corrosion-resistant fluorescent fittings
Medium level of specification (up to 750 lux at workplace)	**Medium level of specification**	
As for Basic above but one luminaire per 6 m².	(As for Basic) non industrial (above)	
Illuminated ceiling: batten mounted fluorescent	(See Suspended ceilings, Medium specification	

fittings fixed to roof or structural floor with suspended ceiling or louvres, open grid panels or translucent panels (see also suspended ceilings, P.52).	p.53, plus Basic non-industrial, above).	

Recessed modular luminaires or downlighters mounted in suspended ceiling grid.	AEG-Telefunken	Multilux recessed range
	Armstrong	Gridmate
	Ascog	Range of recessed modular luminaires
	BBI Lighting	Visolite range of recessed fittings
	C & R Plastics	Modular luminaires and downlighters
	Concord	Range of downlighters
	Courtney Pope	Recessed modular luminaires
	Crompton Parkinson	Modulay
	Edison Halo	Range of downlighters
	Erco	Downlight ranges
	Fluorel	Range of downlighters
	Forma	Range of downlighters
	Hoffmeister	Range of downlighters
	Iris Lighting	Clef range of recessed luminaires
	LDMS	Formalux and range of downlighters
	Lita	Range of downlighters
	Liteway	Range of downlighters
	Lumitron	Range of modular recessed luminaires and downlighters
	Marlin	Range of downlighters
	Martingale	Range of modular luminaires
	Moorlite	Range of modular luminaires
	Philips	Planner range and range of downlighters
	Raak	Multiple Choice range
	RADA & SLR	Recessed Modular Trimless range
	Spectrum	Herbst range of modular luminaires
	Thorn Lighting	Range of downlighters

High level of specification (up to 1500 lux at workplace)

Directional/local lighting with luminaires (tungsten or fluorescent) located anywhere on track; combined with general lighting to give overall lighting with accents. Some integrated systems make provision for signs, power cables, business equipment, telephones, etc.	AEG-Telefunken	Gealux (with continuously mounted plug-in luminaires)
	C & R Plastics	Altalite track and fitting
	Concord	Lylespan track system and range of spotlights; Tubetrack
General or localised lighting: recessed or semi-recessed modular luminaires designed for air handling, mounted in grid of flat or coffered suspended ceiling.	Contact Marketing	Tula tubular system
	Courtney Pope	Display track and fittings
	Edison Halo	Power Trac with range of spotlights
Local task lighting (e.g. adjustable pole mounted; desk mounted, etc) and/or freestanding uplighters.	Erco	Monopoll and other tracks plus range of spotlights
	Flos	Halley tubular lighting system
	Fluorel	Track with range of spotlights

Forma	Dimensione tubular lighting and track sytem
Hoffmeister	Track systems with range of fittings and Multitube system
Oswald Hollman	Kinkeldey 1800 series of lighting systems
Insideout	Track and spotlight systems
Kalmar	Fluor 80 tubular lighting system
LDMS	TI Track, Nokia and Fagerhults track systems and range of fittings; also Supertube system.
Lita Display	Lita track with range of spot lights and Systeme Spacialita
Liteway	Litetrack and range of spotlights
Lumitron	Lumline and range of fittings
Marlin	D Track and J Track with range of fittings
Martingale	Integrated System
Philips	RCS track systems with range of fittings
Raak	Tube-Lite
RADA & SLR	ES 10 tubular lighting system
Thorn Lighting	Programme 2
BBI Lighting	Visolite range of air-handling luminaires
Courtney Pope	Range of air-handling luminaires
Erco	Air-handlingdownlighters
LDMS	Fagerhults range of air-handling luminaires
Lumitron	Range of air-handling luminaires
Martingale	Recessed air-handling luminaires
Moorlite	Air-handling luminaires
Philips	TCS 429
Thorn Lighting	Programme 1
Artemide	Task lights
Best & Lloyd	Range of task lights
Concord	Lytetube task light
Edison Halo	SPI Range task lighting units and uplighters
Erco	Monopoll
Forma	Range of task lights
Hille	Task-Am lighting (see also Furniture and Office Systems, p.100)
Hoffmeister	Multilight suspended task lighting and range of desk fittings
LDMS	Fagerhults Ljuskran system
Raak	Task lite range
Spectrum	Herbst range – task lighting units and uplighters
Thorn Lighting	Range of task lighting and LEOL uplighters

Fire protection

Detectors, alarms and extinguishing devices to protect life and reduce the possible damage to property.

Fires in buildings cause much loss of life and damage to property; it is only sensible to prepare for emergencies by not only selecting the correct type of equipment for the specific risk but also ensuring that it is correctly located in readily available positions. Local fire brigades can usually be approached for expert advice on the appropriate provision for protection. To help determine the type of devices and level of specification the following must be considered/ determined:

Regulations and controls

— Check on the appropriate fire prevention legislation, i.e. either that for new and altered buildings or that for occupied buildings; these deal largely with prevention of spread of fire and lay down standards for materials, costruction, internal planning, etc.
— Check on building regulations and requirements for means of escape and provision of fire fighting equipment. Advice can be obtained from the local authority.
— Check on requirements of fire insurers: these are not necessarily compulsory and some compromise may need to be made, i.e. the cost of the installation will have to be weighed up against possible reduction in annual premium.

Detectors and alarms

— If people are to escape in the event of a fire, and the fire brigade is to arrive in time to contain the blaze, early detection and warning is essential.
— Consider which method will be most suitable:

• Hand-operated alarms, e.g. fire bells or sirens. Disadvantages: outbreak may not be noticed early enough, especially in areas not visited or used regularly; no warning during times that premises are unoccupied; alarm not continuous.

• Manually activated electrical alarm: has some of the disadvantages of the hand-operated type.
• Automatic detectors/alarms: these do not rely on the human element and function day and night. They may be combined with the manually activated types and connected to circuits which will automatically switch off fans or other machines. Various types are available – flammable vapour detectors, different types of smoke detectors, heat detectors, etc. In larger installations a control unit should be considered. Microprocessor types are available which can be programmed to respond in various ways, e.g. sounding alarms; signalling the fire brigade; operating sprinklers or other automatic systems.

Intruder detection devices can be linked to such control units.

Extinguishing devices

— Various types of devices are available and the correct choice will be determined by considering a number of factors, including the sort of fire which is most likely, cost, regulations and insurance requirements.
— Portable fire extinguishers with various agents for a range of risks:

Type of fire	Suitable type of extinguisher
Electrical equipment	Carbon dioxide; dry powder; vaporising liquids
Cellulose materials	Water; foam; carbon dioxide; dry powder; vaporising liquids
Flammable liquids	Foam; carbon dioxide; dry powder; vaporising liquids
Gases or liquid gases	Water
Combustible metals (magnesium, sodium, etc)	Carbon dioxide (limited application); dry powder (special powder)

To avoid confusion in the event of a fire multi-purpose extinguishers may be used. These contain dry powder suitable for most types of fire.
— Wall-mounted hose reels: usually more effective than portable water-type extinguishers. Must be so positioned that every space can be entered and, when fully extended, the hose can reach within 6 m of every part of the space.
— Automatic installations: i.e. grid of water pipes fixed under the ceiling with sprinklers containing a heat-sensitive quartzoid bulb spaced at regular intervals. Bulbs are available which break at temperatures ranging from 68 to 180°C. Heat automatically activates sprinklers in immediate vicinity. The flow of water can be made to work an alarm. Advantages: effective protection in premises involving special risk and reduction in annual fire insurance premium. Disadvantage: may be difficult or impossible to install in existing building.

General considerations

— Must water damage be avoided at all costs? Consider use of dry powder or vaporising liquid extinguishers.
— Consider number and positions of portable extinguishers, hose reels, etc.
— Position of central controls (e.g. alarms, valves and test gear) in the case of automatic sprinkler system. Should be easy to reach and in a relatively prominent place.
— Water supply requirements for hose reels and automatic sprinkler systems. In the case of sprinklers two independent water suppliers may be required.
— Consider system for venting of smoke to

reduce possible hazard and damage. (See under Ventilation, p.72.)

— Consider emergency lighting.
— Determine and compare maintenance procedures required to ensure continued efficacy of appliances and/or installation.

Cost

— Compare installation, maintenance, and in-use costs for the different methods under consideration.

Table 20 Fire protection. Levels of specification and manufacturers.

Basic level of specification	Suppliers and manufacturers	
Manually activated, electrically operated alarm system. Series of switches each installed behind glass, which must be broken to gain access; operation of any one switch sounds all alarm bells and, if required, records on central indicator where alarm was operated.	Anglesey	Break-glass call points
	Blick National	Break-glass call points
	Carters	Manual call points
	Chloride Gent	Model 1102 manual alarm point
	Chloride Standby	Bardic break-glass units
	Hoseworth	Range of manual call points
	I & G	Onguard Manual Call
	Mather & Platt	Manual call points
	Merryweather	Break-glass and hand operated units
	Reliance Systems	Manual call points
	Saft	Break-glass units
	Static Systems Group	Break-glass units
	Tann Synchronome	Manual call points
	Total Fire Protection	Manual call points
	Transcall	Break-glass/manual units
Portable fire extinguishers, water and/or other types, as required for specific risk. Provision at rate of minimum 1–2 of extinguishing capacity for each 250 m^2 of floor area.	Angus	Range of portable extinguishers
	Antifyre	Range of portable extinguishers
	Dunford	Range of portable extinguishers
	Kestral Marketing	Range of portable extinguishers
	L & G	Onguard range of portable extinguishers
	Merryweather	Range of portable extinguishers
	Nullifire	Range of portable extinguishers
	Nu-Swift International	Range of portable extinguishers
	Total Fire Protection	Range of portable extinguishers
Medium level of specification		
Automatic alarm devices operated either by heat or smoke. Detectors spaced so that each will cover an area of between 20 and 100 m^2 and, if required, be connected to a central indicator or control unit.	AFA Minerva	Range of detectors and System 1100
	Anglesey	Range of detectors and control units
	Antifyre	Range of detectors
	Blick National	Detectors and control panels
	Carters	Range of detectors and control units
	Chloride Gent	Range of detectors and control units
	Chloride Standby	Bardic range of detectors and control panels
	Chubb Fire Security	Range of detectors
	Electronic Alarms	Minitwin Fire Control

	Hoseworth	Range of detectors and control units
	L & G	Onguard detection equipment
	Mather & Platt	Range of detectors and control units
	MK Electric	Red Alert range of detectors
	Nu-Swift	Nw Flash Model 7777 (battery operated smoke detector)
	Pyrotector	Smoke Sentinel
	Reliance Systems	Range of detectors and control units
	Static Systems Group	Statiscan detectors and control units
	STC-Electronic Security	Detector systems
	Tann Synchronome	Series 3000 detectors and range of control units
	Total Fire Protection	Range of detectors and control units
	Transcall	Range of detectors and control units
	Walter Kidde	Fireseer and Fire Alert 1201/E
	Zettler	Range of detectors and control units
Wall-mounted 22 m long fire hose reels supplemented by suitable type of portable extinguisher (see under Basic, above).	Angus	Range of hose reels
	Chubb Fire Security	Hose reels
	Dunford	Norsen hose reels
	L & G	Jason and Elgon hose reels
	Merryweather	Range of hose reels
	Nullifire	Range of hose reels

High level of specification

Automatic installation, e.g. sprinklers with turbine operated alarm arranged to repeat at the local fire station. May be connected to a central control unit, possibly microprocessor type. Supplemented by suitable type of portable extinguisher (see under Basic, above).	AFA Minerva	System 700 and other systems
	Fire Security	Automatic sprinkler and waterspray systems
	Haden Fire Protection	Viking sprinkler system
	Mather & Platt	Gas extinguishing systems
	Tann Synchronome	Halon 1301 extinguishing systems
	Total Fire Protection	Automatic sprinkler systems
	Walter Kidde	Halon Fire Suppression System
	Zettler	Automatic extinguishers

Plumbing: toilets and water supply

Sanitary accommodation – room or space containing one or more WC or urinal – and fittings requiring a supply of cold and/or hot water.

The direct provision of sanitary accommodation or the upgrading of existing private facilities – as opposed to the use of shared facilities in a multi-occupied building – is often necessary, e.g. in conversions of older buildings. Specialist advice should be sought but to help decide on the installation and the level of specification, the following must be considered/determined:

Basic considerations

— Determine the minimum requirements for sanitary accommodation as laid down in the relevant regulations, e.g. the Offices, Shops and Railway Premises Act 1963, the Factories Act 1963 and the Building Regulations.
— The following are, generally speaking, minimum requirements and do not necessarily make provision for peak periods of use; allow for more accommodation wherever possible:

● WCs for females and males where no urinals are provided: 1 for 1–15 persons; 2 for 16–30 persons; 3 for 31–50 persons.
● WCs for males where urinals are provided: 1 for 1–20 persons; 2 for 21–45 persons; 3 for 46–75 persons.
● Urinals (1 stall or 600 mm of space): 0 for 1–15 persons; 1 for 16–30 persons; 2 for 31–60 persons.
● Washbasins for males and females: 1 for 1–15 persons; 2 for 16–30 persons; 3 for 31–50 persons. In factories with dirty processes, 1 for every 10 persons.

— How easily can existing/new accommodation be upgraded/installed? In an old building the plumbing and drainage may be difficult and expensive to modify.
— Where can a new installation be located? This will be dictated by the position of existing pipes and ducts, ventilation, room sizes etc.

Sanitary installations

— Will the accommodation be centralised or dispersed? Are there any spaces which require en suite facilities, e.g. directors' suite, reception area, etc? How will this affect or limit future re-arrangement of spaces?
— Consider what type of installation will be most practical/appropriate, e.g. individual fittings or panels with pre-plumbed fittings attached in an existing space, or a completely prefabricated unit.
— If prefabricated units are to be used compare systems in terms of construction, materials (metal, wood, plastic, concrete, etc), partition thickness and strength, etc.
— Decide on type of fittings (e.g. wall hung or floor standing) and on material (e.g porcelain, stainless steel, plastic, etc).
— Decide whether cisterns (for use with urinals) should be concealed or visible.

Water supply

— What fittings which require cold and/or hot water connections are needed? Consider the following:

● Cleaners' sink or robust construction where buckets can be filled and mops and cloths cleaned. There should be one on each floor preferably adjoining a toilet.
● Sink for coffee/tea making facilities.
● Process sink for special use, usually large capacity and of stainless steel.
● Special fittings, e.g. laboratory sinks, possibly with overhead servicing, pumped drainage, etc.
● Shower cubicles which may be part of either toilet or changing accommodation.
● Keep in mind coffee-making machines, water coolers, etc, which may need water connections.
● Will cold water supply be via storage cistern? If so, consider storage requirements and position of drinking water outlets (connected directly to main service pipe).
● Will hot water be required for all or some of the fittings? Consider heating if not from central source (see p.78).

General

— Can sanitary accommodation be adequately ventilated? Must have window or skylight with free area of at least one-twentieth of the floor area or mechanical extraction discharging into the open air (see p.72).
— Consider provision which is suitable for disabled persons, i.e. ambulent disabled and wheelchair users.
— Ascertain most functional fixing heights for fittings, e.g. washbasin 850 mm to rim, WC 400 mm and urinal pods 600 mm to rim.
— Remember that sanitary accommodation may not open directly into a room where people are habitually employed: an intermediate space or lobby must be provided.

Accessories

— Consider what accessories will be required for the various spaces/fittings, e.g:

● Waste bins for disposal of sanitary towels – an incinerator may be required if more than 10 females are employed.
● Mirrors over washbasins.
● Towel dispensers or hot-air dryers and soap dispensers.

Cleaning and maintenance

— Compare fittings for strength, ability to

withstand damage (chipping and scratching) and ease of cleaning – also at junction between fittings and structural surfaces.

— Avoid obstructions – legs, pedestals, exposed pipes, etc – which will make cleaning difficult. Wall-mounted WCs must have enough clearance from floor to make cleaning possible.

— Wall and floor surfaces should be hard wearing, impervious and easy to clean, with all angles and corners covered.

— All cisterns and pipework must be accessible for maintenance and repair.

Cost

— Compare the installation, maintenance and in-use costs for the fittings/units under consideration.

Table 21 Plumbing; toilets and water supply. Levels of specification and manufacturers.

Basic level of specification	Suppliers and manufacturers	
Individual sanitary fittings (WCs, urinals, washbasins) which may be part of a matching range, installed in fully enclosed space.	Anderson Ceramics	Range of sanitaryware
	Armitage Shanks	Range of sanitaryware
	Associated Metal Works	Steristeel urinal slabs and WC pans
	Chloride Shires	Range of sanitaryware
	Concentric	Stainless steel urinals and WC pans
	Dahl	Range of stainless sanitary appliances
	Doulton Sanitaryware	Range of sanitaryware
	DSM Industrial Engineering	Stainless steel urinals
	Ferham Products	Range of sanitaryware
	Fordham Plastics	Range of sanitaryware
	GEC Anderson	Range of stainless sanitary appliances
	Hunting Industrial Plastics	Moulded plastic urinals
	Hygienic Engineering	Urinals
	Ideal Standard	Range of sanitaryware
	Saville	Range of stainless sanitary appliances
	Sissons	Stainless steel urinals
	Twyfords	Range of sanitaryware
Standard stainless steel sink unit with cupboard under and/or heavy duty cleaner's sink (ceramic).	Alan Cooper	Classic and Connoisseur units
	Boulton & Paul	K2P units
	Crosby Kitchens	Octavia units
	Elkins	Sink units
	Gower Furniture	Various units
	Hygena	Various units
	Kalmar Interior	Various units
	Landywood Cabinet	Milliplan units
	Magnet & Southerns	500 and 600 units
	Geo A Moore	Projects units
	Poggenpohl	Various units
	Rippers	Europlan and Cusina units
Medium level of specification		
Pre-plumbed sanitaryware panels and, if required, shower and toilet cubicles installed in fully enclosed space.	Armitage Shanks	IPS System 7 modular range of pre-plumbed units
	Armsil	Prefabricated plumbing units
	Bowater Hills	Consort cubicles
	Cubiform	WC cubicles
	Fordham Plastics	Shower units
	Glynwed	Shower units
	Langley London	Kemmlit cubicles

	Mallinson-Denny	Pantamel and Standard cubicles
	Midland Veneers	Cubicles and toilet partitions
	Plastics Marketing	Plasmarc cubicles and toilet partitions
	Saville	Sancab toilet compartment
	Thrislington	Clene shower and WC cubicles
	Twyfords	Range of pre-plumbed sanitaryware and shower screens and cubicles
	Unilock	Cubicles
	United Storage	Excelsior toilet cubicles
	Venesta International	Toilet and shower compartments
Large capacity heavy duty stainless steel process sinks.	Associated Metal Works	Stainless steel bowls and troughs
	Concentric	Stainless steel cleaners' sinks and wash troughs
	Dahl	Stainless steel sinks
	DSM Industrial Engineering	Range of heavy duty stainless steel sinks with underframes
	Hygenic Engineering	Stainless steel wash troughs
	TRF Pland	Range of industrial sinks with underframes
	Saville	Stainless steel wash troughs

High level of specification

Self-contained, prefabricated toilet unit containing WC and washbasin with main drainage connection.	En-tout-cas	Securra toilet and washroom units
	Makoni Establishment	Feal units
	Mercian	Masterloo
	Portasilo	Portaloo Classic range
	Presco	Steelco and Superloo
	Promotional World	Mero/Rasselstein sanitary units
	Swiftplan	Wet Module units
	Wyseplan	Monoloo
Special drainage fittings for processes with corrosive wastes; overhead connection for sinks requiring location away from drainage points, etc.	Sintacel	Range of laboratory sink units
Standard stainless steel sink with cupboard under combined with electric hobs (or gas burners) and small refrigerator in one compact unit.	John Strand Contracts	Mini-Kitchen

Water heating

Systems and appliances for heating washing water and which are located within the occupied space.

If hot water is required and is not available from a central source (e.g. in a multi-occupancy building) an independent system will be needed. Specialist advice should be obtained, but to help determine the method and equipment to be used, and the level of specification, the following must be considered/determined:

Basic considerations

—   For what purposes will hot water be required, e.g. showers, washbasins, sinks, other?
—   What will the pattern of demand be, i.e. how much water will be required for the different purposes, how regularly will it be used, etc? For hand washing, etc, research has shown that 50–70% savings in water consumption can be made if spray taps are used rather than bib taps, i.e. with spray taps allow 6 l/person/day and with bib taps 3 l/person/day.
—   Will water heating form part of a space heating system (see p.75) or will it function independently?

Source of energy

—   Consider what energy source will be most appropriate. This will be affected by various practical considerations, including availability, storage, flue requirements, capital and/or running costs, etc.
—   Oil, gas and electricity are commonly used for water heating. If fuel is to be used for water heating only, choice will generally be between gas and electricity. Solar radiation is a possible alternative for at least part of the heating requirement, i.e. to supplement a conventional system.

System

—   Which would be most practical and economical: a central system, possibly with storage; local heaters at draw-off points; or a combination of the two? Are fittings/units requiring a hot water supply grouped close together or dispersed?
—   Will it be necessary to provide for storage of hot water? If storage is needed the general rule of thumb for offices and factories is to make provision at the rate of 5 l /person. If not, i.e. if only small quantities of hot water are needed, instantaneous heaters may provide simplest solution.
—   The basic systems are as follows:
●   Combined with space heating, i.e. an indirect hot water cylinder – water heated by boiler is passed through calorifier (coil or tank,

etc) inside cylinder. Cylinder is usually fitted with electric immersion heater as an auxiliary heating source.
●   Indirect hot water cylinder fed by own small boiler.
●   Cistern-type and low-pressure type electric water heaters with thermostatically controlled immersed element
●   Free-outlet electric heater which is able to supply only one fitting.
●   Instantaneous-type heaters (gas or electric) which may be either single outlet or multi-point. Cold water flows through heater when tap is turned on giving continuous supply of hot water. The amount delivered will vary from three pints to two or more gallons per minute and depends on the size and heating capacity of the appliance.
●   Solar collector panels which heat water in hot water cylinder either directly or indirectly (no heat exchanger). An auxiliary heating source will be required as part of normally operating system (e.g. boiler or immersion heater) and which can be switched to take over automatically.
●   Heat pumps: some may be used to heat water (see p.77).

Detail considerations

—   Consider type and location of heating/ storage units relative to the fittings they are to supply, also pipe sizing, to ensure adequate water pressure.
—   What flues, vents, warning pipes and cold water supply cisterns are required for the installation? It may in some cases, e.g. the conversion of an old building, be difficult to provide these and an alternative solution will then have to be found.
—   If solar collectors are to be used, what surface area is needed? Where will they be installed? Can they be mounted at the correct angle (inclination), facing the right direction (orientation)?
—   Will a circulating pump be required for the system and/or any controls, e.g. automatic switching to auxiliary heat source?
—   If instantaneous heaters are used, should they be supplied with swivel spouts or for connection to the hot taps of the fittings?
—   Consider insulation of system to reduce heat loss, i.e. lagging to the cylinder and, possibly, the pipes.

Maintenance

—   How easily can units/appliances be cleaned, serviced and replaced?

Cost

—   Compare the installation, maintenance and in-use costs for the system/equipment under consideration.

Table 22 Water heating. Levels of specification and manufacturers.

Basic level of specification	Suppliers and manufacturers	
Single outlet heaters, either free-outlet electric type or instantaneous heaters (gas or electric).	Aquatron	Sygnet and other ranges (electric, for washbasins and showers)
	Chaffoteaux	Corvec Celt range (gas, for sinks and washbasins), SHIZ (gas, for shower)
	Deltaflow	Showerpack (electric, for shower)
	Dimplex	DXW range (electric, models for washbasin and shower)
	Gainsborough	203 (electric, for sinks or washbasins)
	Gardom & Lock	Alflow (electric, free-outlet type)
	Heatrae-Sadia	Wide range (electric, for sinks, washbasins and showers)
	IMI Santon	Sprite (electric, for shower) and Sanspray (electric, for washbasins), etc
	WH Smith	Dec and UWT ranges
	Stiebel Eltron	DH (electric, for sinks, washbasins and showers)
	Walker Crosweller	Miralec Supreme (electric, for shower)

Medium level of specification		
Multi-point instantaneous type heater (gas or electric).	Chaffoteaux	Corvec Britony II (gas)
	Main Gas Appliances	Main range (gas)
	Prometheus	Leblanc 9 PE (gas)
	WH Smith	BWT range (electric)
	Stiebel Eltron	DH (electric)
	TI Gas Heating	Ascot Sovereign
Electric storage heater – either cistern or pressure type – with thermostatically controlled immersed element or thermostatically controlled gas storage heater. Alternatively, hot water cylinder (direct type) with gas circulator, i.e. unit which heats water which is then stored in, and drawn off from, the cylinder.	HeatraeSadia	Comprehensive range of electrical water heaters
	IMI Santon	Comprehensive range of electrical water heaters
	Johnson & Starley	Janstor (gas-fired)
	Main Gas Appliances	Main Solent (gas-fired circulator)
	Prometheus	Lochinvar (gas-fired)
	Redring Electrical	Storage heaters (electric)
	WH Smith	PWT low-pressure (electric)

High level of specification		
Indirect type hot water cylinder with own small boiler – cylinder may be fitted with immersion heater; boiler may form part of warm air space heating system (see also p.76).	Biddle	Riello Sanitary Water Maker air-to-water heat pump type boiler
	Combat	Range of waste boilers
	Garbutt	Air heaters (can be used to give a hot water supply)
	Harton	Hartonaut heating and hot water units; also preformed plumbing units

	Heatrae-Sadia	Aggressor (oil) and Vendetta (gas) ranges
	Johnson & Starley	Janus (gas-fired)
	Myson	Oil and gas-fired boilers
	Thorn Heating	Oil and gas-fired boilers
	Vaillant	Combi (gas-fired)
	Worcester Engineering	Heatslave and Delgo (gas-fired)
Solar collector(s) used to supplement conventional system (e.g. electric storage heater) or indirect hot water cylinder with own boiler.	Don Engineering	Solar collector panels
	IMI Range	Solar collector panels
	Lennox Industries	SMS 3 Solarmate
	Spencer Solarise	Solar collector panels
	Sun Harvester	Solar heating system
	Sunray	Solar heating system
	Van Leer	Solar collector panels

Ventilation: air extraction

Exchange of inside air with fresh air from outside to provide adequate supply of oxygen, to remove unwanted contamination (e.g odours, smoke, etc) and to keep heat and moisture at acceptable levels. (See also Ventilation: heating, cooling and conditioning, p.75.)
The choice of ventilation (or air-conditioning) system is affected by various factors including the orientation of the building, functional requirements, the degree of flexibility of the accommodation, etc, and specialist advice must be obtained. To help decide on the type of ventilation required and the level of specification the following must be considered/determined:

Natural ventilation

— Can adequate ventilation/air extraction be obtained without resorting to mechanical means? Can one, in other words, rely on opening windows and, possibly, roof ventilators? If so, will this be true all through the year?
— Natural ventilation on its own may not be a satisfactory solution for various reasons:

● The outside air may be too cold during winter months and ventilation must then be combined with heating (see p.75).
● In deep plan buildings or internal rooms (e.g. toilets) where extract fans may be required (see below).
● External pollution and/or noise may prevent the opening of windows.
● The internal environment may need to be carefully controlled, e.g. no dust particles in the air.
● In spaces where offensive or injurious fumes are produced, e.g. laboratories.

Mechanical or forced ventilation

— There are three basic systems of forced ventilation:

● Fresh air supply: air is forced into the space while stale air finds its own way out.

● Air exhaust: stale air is sucked out and replacement air finds its own way in.
● A combination of the first two methods.

— Exhaust is the simplest method and is usually accomplished by using window-mounted and/or roof-mounted extract fans. In some cases (e.g. internal toilets, laboratories, etc) vertical and/or horizontal ducts as well as hoods may be required.

— Fresh air supply systems are usually combined with heating/cooling (see p.75).

Detail considerations

— The amount of ventilation required – which will vary according to the function and volume of the space, local building regulations, etc – must be determined. The following list indicating air changes per hour gives a rough guide to the basic requirements:

	Air changes/hr
Toilets	10–15
Offices	6–8
Laboratories	4–6
Factories	6–10

— The sizes, positions and types of inlets and outlets will affect not only the amount of ventilation but also the pattern of air movement (velocity, direction, etc); correct movement throughout the space is important to ensure a feeling of freshness rather than stuffiness for the occupants. Care must be taken to avoid draughts.
— Consider the need for window mounted extract fans; roof ventilators with or without extract fans; fume cupboards for laboratories; ducting.
— Toxic materials or fumes need a high efficiency, aerodynamically designed fume cupboard, while for non-toxic fumes a lower cost conventional type may be adequate.
— Heat/energy saving; units are available in which the exhaust air passes through a 'heat wheel' and incoming fresh air (passing through a

separate channel) is also forced through the wheel absorbing heat deposited by the extracted air.

Maintenance/durability

— How durable are the components under consideration? How regularly will they need specialised servicing?

— How quietly and smoothly do motors and moving parts operate? How easily can they be maintained and spare parts obtained?

Cost

— Compare the installation, maintenance and in-use costs for the equipment under consideration.

Table 23 Ventilation; air extraction. Levels of specification and manufacturers.		
Basic level of specification	**Basic level of specification**	
Special adjustable vents incorporated into window frames allowing better control of ventilation than that achieved through normal opening lights alone.	Airflow	Nicoll range of ventilators
	Archivent Sales	Novent, Klimalux plus range of other ventilators
	Consoles	Range of natural ventilators (not in window frames)
	Greenwood Airvac	Permavent and Airvac Acoustic Ventilators
	Hinchliffe & Sons	Bonaire ventilator
	Silavent	Freshflo
	R.W. Simon	Ventamatic range
Sealing devices/draughtproofing for use around doors and windows to eliminate unwanted air filtration	Archivent Sales	Various PVC and rubber weather seals
	Douglas Kane	Ellen draught excluders
	Kingdom Marketing	Range of draught strips and weather bars
	Kleeneze	Superseal range of seals
	Manton Insulations	Range of weather and draught seals
	Neilson & Barelay	Wintun weather bars and strips
	Sealmaster	Range of weather and draught seals
	Schlegel Engineering	Guard-seal plus range of other weather seals
	Slottseal	Primo Profile draught strips
	Varnamo Rubbers	Range of weather strips
Roof ventilators providing controllable natural ventilation. Some models have weatherproof blades fitted which open when activated by fire detection systems to aid clearance of smoke; can also be connected to room thermostat to control heating in summer.	Argosy Fenton	Heat-Valve
	Colt International	Meteor, Colville and range of other ventilators
	Greenwood Airvac	Roofline and Plusaire
	JRF Panels	Range of roof ventilators
	Precision Metal Forming	SR Ventilator
	H.H. Robertson	Streamline, Monitor and Fire Ventilators
Medium level of specification		
Extract fans – window-, wall- or roof-mounted. Most models are available with reversible air flow and speed control together with backdraught shutters.	Airflow Developments	
	Colchester Fan	Aidelle Wallfan range
	Dolphin Glass Fibre	Indola range
		Dolfan powered roof ventilator units
	Enviro-Aesthetic	Enviras Clima range (roof exhausters with direct air suction)
	GEC-Xpelair	GX, WX and RX ranges
	Greenwood Airvac	Merchavent
	Myson	Hellix range

	Nu-Aire Philips Small Appliance Roof Units Silavent Vent-Axia Vortice Woods	Range of extract fans Window-mounted fan Maico range Windsor and Continental Universal and Standard ranges Vortaer range GP Propeller Fan range and range of roof extract units
Individual extract fan to internal toilet; connected to exterior wall or roof with 102 mm standard ducting. Can be wired into lighting circuit to operate when light is switched on and may be fitted with electronic timer to run fan for selected period after light is switched off.	Airflow Developments GEC-Xpelair Greenwood Airvac Roof Units Silavent Vortice	Aidelle Loovent range DX 200, DX 200T and TAF 330 Merchavent P and PD Maico range Continental and Mayfair Record Timer range

High level of specification

Heat recovery fan units.	Riga Metal Products Roof Units	Metsovent MNaico Pioneer Units
Roof-mounted extract fan unit connected to central duct zone.	Colt International Enviro-Aesthetic Metair Myson Roof Units VES Andover Woods	Typhoon and Hurricane ranges of powered ventilators Clima roof exhauster with ducted air suction Multivent and other toilet extract units Mechanical ventilators and axial flow fans Europak, Apollo and Venus units Range of duct- or roof-mounted units LMF and MF roof extract units
Ducted fume extract units, e.g. fume cupboard.	Cygnet Joinery Gallenkamp Grant Westfield Miller Williams Morgan & Grundy Sintacel	Range of fume cupboards Fume cupboard Lab 800 fume cupboard Multiflex and MW 1000 fume cupboards Large range of fume cupboards and hoods Aerodynamic and Mobile fume cupboards

Ventilation: heating, cooling and conditioning

Controlling at least the temperature of the fresh air supply and, in the case of air-conditioning, controlling the humidity as well as filtering the air to remove airborne dust and, if required, odours. (See also Ventilation: air extraction, p.72.) The choice and design of a forced ventilation system combined with either heating only or air-conditioning is a complex task and specialist advice must be obtained. To help decide on the method and equipment to be used, and the level of specification, the following must be considered/determined:

Basic strategy

— If a forced fresh air supply system is to be used (as opposed to natural ventilation or a simple mechanical extract system – see p.72) this should be combined with space heating at least. If this is combined with mechanical extraction air can be recirculated at times e.g. in winter to make warming-up in the mornings more rapid. During the summer extracted air is exhausted and only fresh air is delivered to the spaces.
— What fuel should be used in the case of a warm air system – gas, oil or electricity? Will air be heated directly or will a heat exchanger (e.g. water-to-air) be used?
— There are various reasons why a simple warm air system may not be suitable. For example; the moisture content of the heated air may be too low, causing discomfort (dry, sore throats) to occupants; cooling may be required in summer; in some spaces (e.g. computer rooms) the internal environment may need to be carefully controlled. In such cases some form of air-conditioning must be used.

Air-conditioning

— Only unit (or room) air-conditioning is considered here. There are two basic types:

• Self-contained units which are the simplest and cheapest. They are compact and must be installed in an outside wall or window. Disadvantages: limits to positioning and capacity – only very low air pressure can be employed to avoid creating draughts.
• Split system type which have an outdoor condenser unit separated from the air-handling unit which can be situated anywhere within the conditioned space or adjacent to it; ducts and diffusers can be used to distribute the air. Although initial costs are higher, this is a more versatile and efficient method with a higher degree of control.

— Before selecting method or equipment, requirements must be well defined, i.e. intended use of all spaces; number of occupants; standard of comfort required; appliances generating heat internally; special circumstances/needs, e.g. humidity, dust or noise control.
— Once the demand on the system can be calculated, efficiency must be balanced against cost.

Heating

— When heating is needed as part of an air-conditioning system, consider the use of a heat pump. In simple terms this is a special type of air-conditioning unit in which the flow of the refrigerant is reversed, enabling heat to be taken from outside the space and discharged inside to produce some, if not all, of the heat requirement.
— The unique feature of the heat pump is its ability to produce more energy than it consumes, and although capital costs may be 10% greater than for conventional air-conditioning units, savings of up to 40% can be made on heating costs.
— Can the heat pump be sited to take advantage of otherwise wasted heat, e.g. extract air or appliances such as refrigeration condensers?

Detail considerations

— Suitable inlets – grilles or nozzles, etc – must be selected to ensure correct air distribution without draught, noise or other undesirable effects. The positioning of inlets and outlets is also very important.
— Are high levels of illumination (600–1000 lux or more) likely to be used? In such cases luminaires give off heat by convection and overheating can result. When ducted air extraction is being used this could be through the luminaires (see lighting, p.59) with air being exhausted during the summer and recirculated in winter.
— There are a few localised (or task) air-conditioning systems on the market – they are usually combined with furniture systems. If these are considered, remember the following: they are a new development and completed installations should be investigated and evaluated; also, a raised floor will be required.
— Ceiling-mounted variable air volume (VAV) units allow more freedom in usage of space (e.g enclosure or open plan) and leave valuable perimeter space clear. These methods usually require a ducted system.

Maintenance/durability

— How durable are the units under consideration likely to be? How regularly will they need specialised servicing?
— How quietly do the different units run?
— Will spare parts be readily available?

Cost

— Compare the installation, maintenance and running costs for the systems/equipment under consideration.

Table 24 Ventilation; heating, cooling, conditioning. Levels of specification and manufacturers.

Suppliers and manufacturers	Basic level of specification	
Warm air system with small local heating plant and short duct runs. Air is filtered and pumped by a fan through ducts to supply grilles. Units incorporate a time clock control and can be used for ventilation in summer by running the fan only. System can include extract fan with air being exhausted (summer) or recirculated (winter) together with fresh air.	Airheating	Airheat Metrikaire range (oil and gas)
	Biddle	Range of warm air heaters (gas)
	Casair	Space heating and ventilating system
	Cleerburn	Spacewarmer (wood waste)
	Colt	MK1V Turbo-Static Heater (oil or gas)
	Combat Engineering	Range of warm air heaters (oil or gas) including unit heaters
	Dravco	Counterflo (oil or gas) and Directflo (gas) with Energymiser time switch/ thermostat
	Enviro-Aesthetic	Series GG warm air furnaces (gas)
	Garbutt & Sons	Range of warm air heaters (oil or gas) including unit heaters
	Johnson & Starley	Range of warm air gas heaters with Modairflow control
	Lennox	Oil-fired warm air heaters
	William May	80 Series (gas or oil)
	Metair	Multivent range of air handlers
	Millfield Engineering	Warm air heaters
	Myson	Sunflame range (gas or oil) and Unit Heater 8/80 range
	Niche	Mistrale (direct gas fired) air heaters
	Paurmatic	Warm air heaters (oil or gas)
	TI Creda	Range of warm air heaters (electric)
	Wanson	Thermobloc (oil-fired)
	Westwarm	Dantherm air heaters (oil or gas)

Medium level of specification		
Self contained window- or wall-mounted air-conditioning units. Heating and cooling or cooling only.	Biddle	Riello range
	Borg-Warner	York range of room air-conditioners
	Enviro-Aesthetic	Delchi and Clima ranges (including suspended/ horizontal) units
	Qualitair	QPM and QWR ranges
	Searle	Comfort Conditioner range (requires ducting)
	Temperature	Prestair range
	TI Creda	Fairline WS 75/100 and WS 150

High level of specification		
Split system air-conditioning units – heating and cooling or cooling only – or ceiling-mounted variable air volume (VAV) units.	Actair	VAV units
	Barber & Colman	VAV units
	Biddle	Hushflo units

	Denco Miller	DM and Computaire ranges (for computer rooms/laboratories, etc)
	EER	VAV units
	Enviro-Aesthetic	Delchi CR Series and Clima ranges (including suspended/horizontal units)
	Qualitaire	Various ranges (QBU and QCM ranges are ceiling mounted)
	Metaire	Multivent Series A Metricaire modular equipment
	Myson	Supastyle
	Ozonaire	VAV units
	Searle	Solent EV/CS range
	Sound Attenuators	VAV units
	Temperature	Prestairr Pacemaker range (may be mounted horizontally on ceiling)
	TI Creda	Fairline Split System range
	Trox	VAV units
	Waterloo Grille	VAV units
Air-to-air or water-to-air heat pump. Heating and cooling.	Anex	Range of heat pumps
	Biddle	Riello Aermec water-to-water heat pumps
	Borg-Warner	York range of heat pumps
	Carlyle	Heat pump system
	Chieftain	Air-to-water and water-to-water heat pumps
	Climate Equipment	Utopia range of split system heat pump air-conditioners
	Eastwood	Range of heat pumps
	Elemental Resource	Ergo air-to-water heat pumps
	Enviro-Aesthetic	Delchi split system heat pumps
	Glynwed	Crusaver range of air-to-water heat pumps
	Lennox	Fuelmaster Plus system (combined with oil-fired warm-air heater)
	Myson	Air-to-water heat pumps
	Searle	Solent RPH heat pumps
	Temperature	Versa Temp
	Toshiba	Range of heat pumps (including window or through-the-wall units)
	Trace	Range of heat pumps
Localised (or task) air-conditioning (see also Furniture: office systems, p.98)	Ackermann	Klimadrant (see also Technodrant under Power supply: trunking, P.59)
	Faram	Superalfa furniture system provides for linking workstations to air-conditioning system
	Steelcase Strafor	Furniture systems provide for linking workstations to air-conditioning system

Heating

Local heating by units 'fired' directly and located within the occupied space. (See also Ventilation: heating, cooling and air-conditioning, p.75.) The amount of heating required in any given space is related to the comfort of the occupants. Conditions are dependent not only on the air temperature and that of the surrounding surfaces, but also on the relative humidity and air movement. Specialist advice should be obtained. To help decide on the method and equipment to be used, and the level of specification, the following must be considered/determined:

Conservation through insulation

— Space heating is the major component of energy use in buildings. Consider energy conservation measures – these will also help to reduce fuel bills.
— Can heat loss from the space in question be reduced through insulation of the roof and/or outside walls and windows? Also by eliminating air leaks to the outside through gaps around badly fitted doors and windows?

Heating requirements

— Determine requirements for each type of space. Unoccupied spaces – passages, lobbies and non-work areas – should not be heated to the same degree as occupied spaces.
— Consider the effects of lighting, people and any heat generating appliances when calculating requirements. Lighting, for example, can provide a considerable proportion of the heating needed, e.g. almost all the heat from a suspended fitting enters the space and in the case of surface-mounted and recessed fittings it is about 80 and 50% respectively.
— Will local heating be the only source of heat or will it be used to supplement a central system, e.g. during intermediate seasons and short, unexpected cold spells? Local heating has the advantage of flexibility.

Source of energy

— Consider what source of energy will be most appropriate. The choice will be affected by various factors, including availability, capital and running costs, local planning requirements, fuel handling and storage.
— The fuels most commonly used for direct heaters are oil, gas and electricity. Solar radiation is a possible alternative for at least part of the heating requirement, but high capital costs, climatic conditions in the UK (where cloudy days outnumber the fine days) and the lack of inexpensive, relatively simple methods of heat storage are problems which still need to be satisfactorily overcome.

System

Consider what type of heat emitters will be used:

● Convectors: the heat is transferred by airflow between the source and the space. Two types are available: natural draught or fan-assisted.
● Radiators: the heat is transmitted directly from the source. Three main types are available: high temperature, which operate at red heat; medium temperature, which are too hot to touch comfortably; and low temperature.
● Thermal storage: units are heated during the night (off-peak) and give off heat during the following day. Block storage heaters consist of heating elements embedded in heat storage material (e.g. refractory bricks) enclosed by an insulated casing. They are not very controllable – heat output drops during the day – are relatively bulky and very heavy. Models combining a fan, usually controlled by a thermostat, are also available.
● Underfloor heating is another method of storing heat, with a grid of cables embedded in a thicker-than-usual screed. This is not as flexible as separate convectors or radiators and can result in overheating during intermediate seasons.
● Ceiling heating: consists of low temperature radiant elements laid above the ceiling over the greater part of the space to give an even distribution. The space above the heating elements must be very well insulated to avoid excessive heat transfer/loss upwards.

General considerations

— Where should the heating units be located? Keep in mind layout of furniture and workstations, positions of windows, etc.
— How adaptable is the system? What will happen if layout is altered? Will system be suitable in both cellular and open-plan office spaces?
— Consider appearance of units. Will they be compatible with overall scheme for interior decor?
— Flexibility and control: to what degree can units be adjusted or controlled to maintain comfortable conditions? For example, room thermostats which respond to heat gains from lighting, occupants and machines, and control the heat output of the units; these can be used in conjunction with time switches to provide programmed heating.
— How easily can units be cleaned, serviced and replaced.

Cost

Compare the installation, maintenance and in-use costs for the different types of equipment under consideration.

Table 25 Heating. Levels of specification and manufacturers.

Basic level of specification	Suppliers and manufacturers	
Wall-mounted draught type convector heaters (gas or electric). Can be thermostatically controlled.	Bray Chromalux	Natural convection heaters
	Claudgen	Warm-zone
	Dimplex	DC20 electric heaters
	Ekco	Convector heaters
	Eltron	Eltrorad convectors
	Philips Small Appliance	Range of wall mounted convectors
	Prometheus	Range of convector heaters (gas-fired with flue)
	Redring	Sunfan
	Unidare	Convector heaters
	Valor	Range of radiant convectors (gas)
Wall mounted radiant type heaters.	Chieftain	Skandarad panel radiators and Radisil infra-red heaters
	Claudgen	Twin-zone
	Dimplex	PCL and Oil-filled Electric ranges
	Ekco	Radiant heaters
	Philips Small Appliance	Range of wall-mounted radiators and radiants
	Redring	Sunstrip tubular heaters
	TI Creda	Range of panel heaters
	Unidare	Panel radiators
Medium level of specification		
Fan type, thermostatically controlled convector heater (gas or electric). Noise may be a problem with this type.	Bray Chromalux	Fan heaters
	Bush Nelson	Inca fan heaters
	Chieftain	Axiatherm range of fan heaters
	Claudgen	Flow-zone and Heat-zone
	Ekco	Fan heaters
	Eltron	Eltroflow fan heaters
	Hanovia	Turboflo fan heaters
	Philips	Fan assisted convector
Ceiling type radiant heating units; thermostatically controlled.	Burgess	Ceiling heating
	ESWA	Ceiling heating
	Thermaflex	Flexel radiant heating system
Underfloor heating with time switch and thermostatic control.	BICC	XLPE floor heating
	Elfidol	Floor heating
	HCP	Floor heating

High level of specification		
Block storage heaters with fan which can be time switched and thermostatically controlled.	Bush Nelson Dimplex Storad TI Creda Unidare	Industrial heaters DA and SC ranges Range of storage heaters TSR range WF range
Special industrial type radiant heating units.	Chieftain Claudgen Colt Combat Eltron Grayhill Westcott Parkinson Cowan Phoenix Burners Redring Schwank	Industrial Radisil Screen-zone TRS15 radiant gas heater Radiant tube heaters (gas-fired) Eltrowave infra-red heaters Blackheat gas heaters Flamrad gas heaters Nor-Ray-Vac gas heaters Sunzone II-Range (electric) 2000 Series infra-red gas heaters

INDEPENDENT COMPONENTS

Screens (heavy duty)

Lightweight, non-loadbearing freestanding divisions to form barriers or enclosed areas in industrial-type spaces.
Proprietary industrial screening/partitioning is available in various construction systems, i.e. stud/sheet, frame/panel, panel/panel (for a description of these methods, see Partitions, p.48). Before deciding on a system and level of specification the following must be considered/determined:

Function

— What is screening required for – security, safety, privacy, as a boundary, to conserve heat, or to act as a barrier to noise, dust and fumes?
— What type of infill will best suit these needs – welded mesh, glass (clear, obscure, reinforced, etc), metal or other sheet material?

Flexibility

— Is flexibility important? Are screens likely to be moved fairly regularly, say, once in each 12–24 months? Some systems are not easy to demount.
— Check on the range of standard modular elements available as part of the system. The larger the range of sizes and types of elements, the greater the flexibility of design.

Construction

— How robust is the construction? Can it withstand possible impact any vehicle used in the space or by material being carried?
— Can screening be dismantled and re-assembled to another configuration without specialist assistance?
— Will a roof/ceiling be required? If so, is anyone likely to walk on it or store materials on it? The roof construction of some systems is not intended to be loadbearing.

General considerations

— What degree of fire resistance and/or sound insulation is required?
— What level of thermal transmittance is acceptable?
— If a high level of performance is required in any or all of these aspects, special care must be taken when selecting a system.
— To what degree will services – lights, switches, power points, etc – be required in the screened area? If these are built into screening, flexibility will be greatly reduced. Use can be made of trunking (see p.57).
— Consider the types of openings needed – doors, windows, hatches, ventilators.
— Must surfaces of screens be capable of use for storage?

Finishes

— Consider suitability of finishes in terms of impact resistance; maintenance and cleaning; sound absorption and appearance.
— Are screens likely to be subjected to damp or humid conditions, or to corrosive fumes? If so, ascertain which finishes will be suitable for the specific conditions.

Cost

— Compare the installation, maintenance and in-use costs for the systems under consideration.

Table 26 Screens, heavy-duty. Levels of specification and manufacturers.

Basic level of specification	Suppliers and manufacturers	
Freestanding screens. Metal faced with doors, glazing, grilles and hatches available.	Ealing	Security screens
	P.C. Henderson Ltd	Workshield
	Industrial Equipment	Sectional Partitioning
	MGK	Industrial partitioning
	Norwood	Easiscreen and President 1
	Paxwood	Conderscreen 875
	Spaceway Design	Industrial partitioning
	Thrislington	SP partitioning
Medium level of specification		
Freestanding screens. Metal or plasterboard faced. Various openings available. May form enclosed rooms; roof/ceiling can be supplied if required.	British Gypsum	Gyproc GMS Enclosure Unit
	Cashman Erectors	Angle Frame
	Conder Group	Conder partitioning
	Dexion	Simplan
	Down & Francis	Easerect works partitioning
	Ealing	Industrial partitioning
	Electrolux	Elux – Partition 900
	L & D Installations	Minor range
	Roneo Vickers	Artisan Industrial
	Steel Equipment Co	Seco single skin industrial partitioning
	Unistruct	Warwick Industrial
	United Storage	Able partitioning
	Wakefield	Humber steel partitioning
	Wellconstruct	New Industrial and Cleanline

Screens (light duty)

Freestanding, easily movable divisions used to provide fully enclosed, semi-enclosed or work group spaces are required in open-plan/landscaped-type office areas.

If some or all of the office space provided is of the open-plan type, i.e. large area in which staff of various levels of responsibility work together without fixed dividing walls, screening of one kind or another will almost certainly be required. To help decide on the appropriate system and level of specification the following must be considered/determined:

Basic strategy

— To establish priorities and help determine the type of spaces required for different functions, groups and individuals consider:

● The amount of work which flows through the office between individuals and groups, and how this happens.

● The frequency of movement and communication which takes place between individuals and groups. A useful way of doing this is to prepare a relationship diagram.

● The degree of association or enclosure required by the various individuals and groups involved. What groups or individuals are involved in confidential work? For which is

privacy essential?

● What tasks or equipment generate noise or distraction of another kind?

● Other factors, e.g. security, supervision, etc.

Flexibility

— If it is important to have a high degree of flexibility of not only work flow and circulation but also of rearranging layouts, groupings, etc, an open-plan/landscaped area may be the solution; if not, see Partitions, p.48. Weigh the requirement for flexibility against the degree of enclosure required by individuals and working groups, and the possible distractions resulting from surrounding movement and noise in this type of space.

— Is the provision of environmental services suitable for an open-plan arrangement? The lighting, heating, and ventilation, as well as the electricity and telephone supplies, may not be as flexible as the system of screening.

Screen function

— Are screens to be used simply for defining work areas or circulation routes and entries to work areas? Alternatively, must they be able to support certain fittings or be part of an integrated furniture system? (See also Furniture: office systems, p.98).

Construction

— Are screens under consideration self-supporting? Are legs fixed or adjustable, i.e. can height of individual screens be varied?

— Can screens be linked? Is this standard or are linking devices fitted as an optional extra? Are the units rigid when assembled? How easily can they be assembled, demounted and moved?

— Can screens support pinboards, shelving and other fittings? Is a range of integrated fittings available? Are the screens part of a completely integrated furniture system?

— Do the screens make provision for wire management, both vertical and horizontal? If so, is the system 'clip-on' or 'lay-in'? How simple and accessible is the system?

— Do the materials and the construction appear to be sufficiently durable and robust to withstand wear and tear, movement and storage?

General considerations

— Is there a range of widths and heights available? Can the system meet the flexibility required for different sizes of workstations and layouts? Are flat, curved, and glazed screens available as part of the system? At least one manufacturer now has a screen system which forms a complete enclosure – a box within a box – which is reasonably mobile.

— Are there any possible hazards, e.g. fire, projecting legs, sharp edges or corners, etc?

— Consider the effect they may have on the environment standards of the office. Will they interfere with the heat distribution, ventilation or lighting?

— What are the acoustic properties? Are screens sound absorbent? A reasonable degree of sound reduction should be possible.

Finish and maintenance

— Consider textures and colours available. Is range wide enough to be compatible with other systems used, e.g. furniture?

— Are surfaces compatible with functional requirements, e.g. glare reducing and/or use as pinboard?

— Can surfaces be easily cleaned and maintained? How easy is it to restore or replace finishes?

— Will legs cause damage to or impressions on carpeting or other floor surfaces?

— Consider appearance, type, and colour of edge trim; also finish to metal parts, e.g. legs, brackets, etc.

Cost

— Compare the installation, maintenance and in-use costs for the systems under consideration.

Table 27 Screens, light-duty. Levels of specification and manufacturers.

Basic level of specification	Suppliers and manufacturers	
Freestanding screens. Fabric covered and sound absorbent. Accessories (e.g. pinboards, shelves, coat hooks, etc) are available with some of the systems.	Abbot Bros	Abbess straight and curved screens
	Click Systems	KDS Display Screens
	Canonairn	Freestanding screens
	Dufaylite	Pinnacle screens
	Ergonom Distributors	Landscape and Panorama ranges
	Flexiform	Kasparian BKD straight and curved screens
	Form International	Freestanding straight and curved screens
	Hille	Mobile screens
	Interfinish	Category I freestanding screens
	Moveable Drywall	Dwarf Walls
	A. Murray	Straight and curved screens
	Office Contracts	Trio Moduli screens
	Open-Plan	Acoustic Screen straight and curved
	Project Office Furniture	Range of screens
	Vickers Furniture	RMF straight and curved screens
	Wiltshier	All Steel straight and curved screens
	Woodspring	Scatter Screens 4000 Range and 5000 Range

Medium level of specification

Freestanding combination/linked screens. Sound absorbent. Compatible with storage units and furniture, and with a limited range of clip-on accessories. Can be glazed.	Abbot Bros	Abbess linked screens
	Arrange Marketing	Interparavent screens
	Canonairn	Linked screens
	Dufaylite	Pinnacle linked screens
	Ergonom Distributors	Misura screens
	Interfinish	Category 2 screens
	Martela	Linked screens
	A. Murray	Linked screens
	Martin Neil Designs	Nobo screens
	OAST	Work station system
	Office Contracts	Trio Moduli screens
	Open-Plan	Range 202 screens
	William Plumkett	Screenform screens
	Tan-Sad	Uniton screens
	Voko	Section screens
	Woodspring	Combination screens 6000 Range and 7000 Range

High level of specification

Freestanding combination/linked screens. Sound absorbent. With wide range of integrated accessories including worktops, storage units and service concealment elements. Range of heights. May form enclosed room. Can be glazed.	Arenson International	Genesis screen system
	Arrange Marketing	Planmobel screen system
	Click Systems	Office Screen range
	Continental Comfort	King screens
	Alan Cooper	System Screens
	Facit	Screen system
	Grant International	Gispen TP screens
	G.A. Harvey	Screen systems
	Hille	Storage Screens
	Intercraft	NUB Range screen system
	Interfinish	Category 3 screens
	Isoplan	Screen system
	Kerrison Furnishing	Marcadet Option screens
	Lucas Furniture	Programme screens
	Matthews	MD Acoustic System screens
	Herman Miller	Action Office Panels and Super Room mobile enclosure
	NKR	Environmental Screen System
	OMK	Screen system
	Open-Plan	Range 303 screens
	Plumb Contracts	PSO screens
	Project Office Furniture	4000 Range screens
	Scott Howard	USM and Castelli Pert screens
	Sisk	Series 3 screens
	Swedeline	Kuppla screens
	Unit 4	TM Box screens
	Vickers Furniture	RMF panel system
	Grant Westfield	KI Cumulus screens
	Wiltshier	All Steel screens

Floor finishes

Material covering sub-floor and providing walking surface.

The range of available floor finishes in tile, sheet and jointless types is extremely diverse and only a few selected materials are included here. Before deciding on the type of flooring and level of specification the following must be considered/determined:

Basic requirements

— What criteria (performance, cost, appearance) must the floor coverings for the different types of area meet? Will the floor, for example, have to withstand abrasion and dirt? Resist heavy tracking? Resist static shock? Provide access to underfloor services?
— What type of sub-floor is the covering to be laid on? The quality of the sub-floor will affect the appearance, wear and life of the covering.

Resistance to wear

— How much wear and tear is the floor expected to have? For extremely heavy wear a very hard surface, such as epoxy screed or end grain woodblock, may be required. The resistance to abrasion can be improved in some materials by the application of a surface hardener.
— The possibility of uneven wear must be borne in mind. Can sections of the material(s) under consideration be replaced easily without relaying the entire floor?

Slipperiness

— Relatively non-slip finishes are usually desirable in most locations. If the floor is likely to be regularly moist or oily, care must be taken as some materials (e.g. rubber and PVC) can be particularly hazardous.

Sound

— Soft floor finishes can contribute to the absorption of airborne sound in a room and will, in addition, absorb impact sound. Heavy carpets with underlay are most effective.
— The floor finish will not have much effect in reducing transmission of airborne sound through the floor; this depends more on the construction and mass of the main floor.

Cleaning and maintenance

— Consider the dirt resistance of the finish. How much effort will be required to keep the floor looking good?
— It is possible to apply a special treatment (e.g. a sealant) which will be effective in protecting the surface and making cleaning easier?
— What materials and equipment will be required for cleaning and maintenance?

Special considerations

— Will the floor be required to carry heavy loads, point loads or wheeled traffic? If so, a floor which is resistant to damage from this type of loading and to impact from shock loading will have to be used, e.g. epoxy resin, end-grain woodblock, etc.
— Are floors likely to come into regular contact with chemicals, fats, etc? No floor finish will be resistant to all the possible combinations; epoxy finishes and vitrified ceramic tiles bedded and jointed with chemical resistant mortar will be suitable for most areas.
— If underfloor heating is to be used check whether the finishes under consideration will effect the heat emission or be effected by the heat.
— The resistance of the material to the build up of static electricity may be an important consideration in certain areas, e.g. computer rooms, as static electricity can cause damage to the micro-circuits; an anti-static finish must be used.

Comfort and appearance

— The hardness and 'warmth' of the respective finishes should be compared. Floor covering without any resilience may be tiring to stand on or walk on for long periods.
— Consider the overall effect required in terms of colour, texture and the treatment of adjoining surfaces. How well will the material retain its appearance in the long term?

Cost

— Compare the installation, maintenance and in-use costs for the finishes under consideration. The length of life and ease of replacing part or all of the floor covering must be assessed in relation to the initial cost.

Table 28 Floor finishes. Levels of specification and manufacturers.

Basic level of specification	Suppliers and manufacturers	
PVC/vinyl sheeting or tiles – mainly a PVC (polyvinyl chloride) resin binder with varying proportions of fillers, pigments, stabilisers, etc. Some PVC floor materials are reinforced with silica quartz grains and others have a backing layer of fibre, cork, foam or some other material to improve the resilience. The degree of resistance to wear varies and depends on high or low percentage of PVC content and thickness of material.	Altro	Acoustic, Safety Tread etc
	Amtico	Range of vinyl tiles
	Armstrong Cork	Arlon, Brigantine, etc
	DLW	PVC Flooring
	Dunlop Semtex	Semflex, Durlon, etc
	Dynamit Nobel	Mipolam
	Forbo-Krommenie	Golovinyl, Colo Rex and Sure Step ranges
	Gerland	Gerflex ranges
	Halstead	Polyflor, Polytred and Polyflex ranges
	W.M. Leaf	Tarolay, Taradal and Taraflex
	Marley Floors	Marleyflex, Vylon, Vynatred, etc
	Nairn	Nairnlay and Crestaflex
	Rieber	Rikett range
	Tarco	Multiflor
Carpet tiles in man-made fibres (e.g nylon, polyester, etc) used alone or in blends (e.g. 50% nylon, 50% polyester). Loose laid tiles have possible advantages: can be rotated to even out wear; individually damaged tiles can be replaced; access to underfloor services is possible.	Anglian	Hercules, Dakar, etc
	Burmatex	Velour, 1000 Antistatic
	Carpets International	Range of carpet tiles
	Checkmate	Range of carpet tiles
	DLW	Polo and Strong
	Dunlop Semtex	Range of carpet tiles
	Esco	Range of carpet tiles
	Karl Ebyl	Isofloor
	Floor Finishes	Computread range
	Freudenberg	Noraflor
	Gaskell Broadlook	High Level and Norsemen
	Halstead	C40–20
	Heckmondwike	Iron Duke
	Heuga	Range of carpet tiles including computer range
	Illingworth	Villatex range
	Littner Hampton	Range of carpet tiles
	Marley Floor	Dekortile and Grandstand
	Nairn	Nairnflair
	Tretford	Tretford range
	Tufted Carpet Tile	Tuca
Medium level of specification		
Carpet tiles – 100% wool or 80% wool, 20% nylon.	Anglian	Regina
	Heuga	415 elite and 420 Shetland (100% wool), Berber (80/20% wool/nylon) and Superlom 80/20% wool/nylon) computer range

Plastic mat or vinyl ribbed duckboarding:
provides useful solution in certain areas, e.g.
workshops, laboratories, etc. Surface raised
above floor level. Hard wearing and provides
insulation as well as a non-slip surface.

High level of specification

Hard wearing jointless industrial type finishes, e.g: Latex screeds in which the binder is rubber latex (natural or synthetic) and Portland or high alumina cement with aggregates (various types are used), pigments and fillers. — Epoxy resin screeds. This type of flooring is, generally speaking, non-dusting with some resilience and can be made non-slip; resistance to water, chemicals, oils, etc, is good.	Cementation Chemicals CBP Colas Dunlop Semtex Elgood Goldschmidt GRAB Resins International Paint Kittridge Lamacrest Prodorite Ronacrete Rowan & Boden Sealocretel Sika Contracts Structoplast Toffolo Tretol Watco	Quickmast 301 Nitoscreed and Nitogrip Weardeck and Safedeck Fleximer Various epoxy finishes Reinau epoxy jointless Epoxy resin flooring Interguard range of epoxy flooring Dex-o-Tex Cheminert (epoxy) and Neotex (latex) Decorerest Epoxy and latex flooring Epoxy and latex flooring Aranbee Epoxy and latex flooring Epoxy and latex flooring Epoxy and latex flooring Epoxy resin flooring Tretoflor Epoxy resin flooring
Hard wearing finishes in tile or panel form, e.g. end-grain woodblock and ceramic tiles, with properties similar to those described for the finishes described above.	Armitage Shanks Philip Cecconi Duro Paviors Fritztile Hewetson Johnson Tiles Langley London Pilkington's Tiles Daniel Platt Quilgotti Reed-Harris Toffolo Jackson	Range of ceramic tiles Ceramic and terrazzo tiles Ceramic and terrazzo tiles Range of terrazzo tiles Anvil end-grain woodblock Range of ceramic tiles Range of ceramic tiles Dorset range Ferrolite ceramic tiles Range of terrazzo type tiles Ostara and Monoceram ceramic tiles Range of terrazzo tiles

Mezzanine floors

Freestanding platforms, usually of structural
steel, which may be used for storage, assembly,
production or office accommodation.
Mezzanine floors provide a way of gaining
additional floor space in areas with relatively
large floor to ceiling heights, and are self
supporting structures as opposed to the
platforms which form part of a multi-tier shelving
system (see p.109). To help decide on the type
of structure required, the following must be
considered/determined:

Need and function

— Would additional floor space be useful? If
so, for what purpose is it needed? If, for storage
only, would a multi-tier shelving system (see
p.109) be a simpler and less costly solution?
Alternatively, consider installing a prefabricated
unit (see p.90) internally – the roof could be used
for long-term storage of relatively lightweight
materials.
— Is the floor to ceiling height in part (or all) of
the premises sufficiently high – around 4.5–5 m
minimum – to install a mezzanine floor? If so, a
freestanding platform will help to utilise the
unused space to ceiling height without
expensive structural changes.

General considerations

— Check whether it is necessary to apply for

local authority approval? If so, determine what their requirements are. Are there any specific fire regulations which will affect the design or the construction?

— What weight will the platform have to carry? Is the existing floor structure strong enough to take the extra point loads?

— What area of platform can be accommodated in the space? What will the best location be, keeping in mind existing columns, doors and windows; circulation routes and access points; and the electrical installation, i.e. lighting and power points on the platform and/or lighting for the area below?

Design and construction

— Consider what clear height will be required under the platform structure. Will this plus the depth of the structure leave enough headroom above the platform?

— Where will the best position be for the staircase, inside or outside the platform?

— The loading the platform is required to carry will affect either the design of a custom-made structure or the choice of a standard unit, e.g. spacing and size of supports. The spacing of columns may be important to ensure maximum unimpeded usable floor space below. Is any specific spacing essential?

— Where is the platform to be located? This may influence the design, e.g. to ensure stability and rigidity of an 'island' platform additional bracing may be required.

— Will the platform be used to provide workspace? If so, must it be enclosed with partitioning or left open with a handrail? Will it be used for storage? If so, how will goods be lifted, i.e. will some of the guardrail need to be removable or will safety-type loading gates be needed? What type of decking will be most suitable – open metal planking/grating or a solid floor of wood (chipboard or plywood) or steel?

Flexibility

— How easily and economically can the systems under consideration be extended?

— Do they have a reasonably wide range of matching components, e.g. alternative decking materials, fascias, loading gates, stair treads (wood and steel), partitioning, etc? Can these be easily added if required at a later date?

Safety

— Are the staircases wide enough and not too steep? Are the treads non-slip?

— Consider provisions for fire protection, i.e. to the underside of the decking and framework. Will an escape cat-ladder be required?

Appearance and finish

— Compare the overall appearance of the systems under consideration and their compatibility with the general interior design concept. If partitioning is to be used, how compatible is it – in terms of appearance, finish, etc – with the platform itself?

— What standard finishes and colours are available? Will finishes be able to withstand normal wear and tear without being easily chipped, scratched, etc? Can surfaces be easily cleaned and maintained?

Cost

— Compare the installation, maintenance and in-use costs for the systems being considered.

Table 29 Mezzanine floors. Levels of specification and manufacturers.		
Basic level of specification	**Suppliers and manufacturers**	
Simple, open mezzanine floor independent of main structure with stairway, handrailing and deck of T & G flooring grade chipboard.	Burton's Structural Engineers	Mezzanine floors
	Gascoigne Engineering	Freestanding storage platforms
	Henderson Safety Tank	Slimline and traditional systems
	Key Industrial Equipment	Mezzanine platforms in extendable modules
	Link 51	Handy Angle Link-Dek and Bottles systems
	Mavil	Maviangle system
	MGK	Raised storage platforms
	Promotional World	ALU-rapid adjustable platform floor system
	Sale Steelform Partitions	Steelform mezzanine platforms
	Southern Storage Systems	Storage floors
	Spaceway Design	Custom made mezzanine floors
	Welconstruct	MM system

Medium level of specification		
Open mezzanine floor system with wide range of components, independent of main structure. With stairway, cat-ladder, safety-type loading gate and decking of open steel planking/grating or timber.	Burton's Structural Engineers	Mezzanine floors
	Dexion	Stordex
	Henderson Safety Tank	Slimline and traditional systems
	Spaceway Design	Custom made mezzanine floors
	Wakefield Storage Handling	Upadek
	Welconstruct	Custom made storage and platform floors

High level of specification		
Enclosed mezzanine floor with compatible partitioning system.	Henderson Safety Tank	Slimline with partitioning
	Key Industrial Equipment	Mezzanine platforms with Keytex partitioning
	Spaceway Design	Mezzanine floors with Industrial or Executive partitioning
	Welconstruct	Custom made platform floors with Welex (or other) partitioning, and P & P range of elevated offices

Material handling: lifting equipment

Equipment for loading bays or decks and for moving goods vertically between floors either internally or externally.

It is important to consider not only production and storage equipment but also that required for transport, for the efficient loading and unloading of goods and, where applicable, its vertical movement between the ground level and upper floors. To help decide on the equipment and level of specification the following must be considered/determined:

Basic strategy

— What type of loads have to be moved, i.e. size, shape, weights, etc? How regularly will these loads be moved?
— How are materials delivered, unloaded and loaded? Do materials have to be moved vertically, e.g. from ground level to first floor storage and/or vice versa? Are there adequate facilities for these operations?
— Would some form of lifting device not only save work and time but also afford better protection for goods during movement? Would it fit into any overall material handling system that the organisation may have?

Loading Bays

— Do the premises have an existing loading bay? If not, is there a suitable location for one? Consider position of storage facilities, production line and external factors, e.g. service roads, manoeuvring area, etc.
— Are there existing loading platforms or, alternatively, could one be added? Consider the height of the platform in relation to vehicle-bed heights. As vehicles vary considerably some form of adjustable dock leveller is usually required, e.g:

• Flush folding: the simplest type – basically just a folding metal bridge between the platform and vehicle – which may be used where no great variance in vehicle-bed heights is anticipated.
• Permanent adjustable: these are built into a pit in the platform and may be either mechanical or hydraulic in operation. The length of the leveller is vital since it determines the angle of incline into and out of vehicles; under no circumstances should the incline be more than 15%.

Weather protection

— Are loading bays/platforms flush with outside walls? Consider the problems of gaps between the vehicles and the building during loading and unloading in terms of energy conservation (i.e. heat loss and cold air entering the plant and offices), exclusion of rain, etc.
— Consider some form of shelter. While a canopy will give protection against rain, etc, it will not solve the problem of energy conservation. Various forms of loading bay shelters are available which seal against the outer surface of the vehicle body.

Elevating docks

—   If it is not possible to install a raised platform – e.g. when converting an existing building and/or when the floor is at ground level – consider using a static (built-in) elevating dock or lift-table.
—   Will it be possible to form a pit of required size and depth in the correct location?
—   Compare the optional extras provided by the various manufacturers, e.g. platform safety edges, handrails, safety bellows or sheet metal side guards, etc.

Goods lifts

—   Is regular vertical movement of goods a problem? Consider the possibility of installing a simple goods lift.
—   What size of car, cage or platform will be required? How heavy will the loads be and how high must they be moved?
—   Consider which type of lift will be most suitable:
●   Electric traction-type – headroom will be required for a machine room.
●   Hydraulic-type – ideal where headroom is confined but a shallow pit will be required. The motor/pump unit can be located up to 30 m away from lift if necessary.
●   Scissors-type lift or platform raised and lowered by motor driven screw – for moving loads over short vertical distances, e.g. between two floors.
—   Should lift be self-contained, i.e. with self-supporting frame? If so, what type of cladding will be required, e.g. weatherproof, open mesh, etc? Alternatively, is brick shaft available or is a loadbearing wall required?

General

—   What are the power requirements for the equipment under consideration? Is 3-phase electrical supply either preferred or essential?
—   Determine what mandatory safety regulations apply to the proposed installation.
—   Assess reliability of all equipment. What type of maintenance/servicing contract (if any) do the manufacturers offer?

Cost

—   Compare the installation, maintenance and in-use costs for the equipment under consideration.

Table 30 Material handling; lifting equipment. Levels of specification and manufacturers.

Basic level of specification	Suppliers and manufacturers	
Flush folding type dock leveller permanently attached to front edge of loading platform.	Becker Lifts Evans Lifts	Serco hinged tip ramp Range of Hunter spring operated and hinged dock boards
	Hafa	PO and PS spring loaded dock levellers
	Stokvis	Range of Kelley front-of-dock levellers
Scissors lift or motor driven screw-type platform possibly with wire mesh protective surround.	Becker Lifts Evans Lifts Gascoigne Engineering	Scissor lifts Hunter lift tables Range of scissor lift tables
	Gough & Co Hi-Lo Leiston Engineering Lodlifta	Scissor lifts Scissor lifts Topper lift tables Tweeny (screw-type) lifts
Medium level of specification		
Elevating dock installed in shallow pit; maximum height approximately 1.5 m. For loading and unloading of vehicles.	Evans Lifts Gascoigne Engineering Hi-Lo Leiston Engineering Power Lift Engineering Stokvis	Hunter Vanloader and Truckloader ranges Range of elevating docks Range of lift tables Topper range of lift tables Range of dock lifts Range of lift tables
Self-contained mechanical or hydraulic-type lift with self-supporting metal framework and wire mesh or blockboard protective surround.	Charnock Lift Services Gascoigne Engineering	Rack-and-pinion goods lift Range of goods lifts

	Husbands	Balmatic document and service lifts
	Lift a Hoist	Microlift service and manual hoists
	Oakland Elevators	Document, service and trolley lifts
	Stannah Lifts	Trolley Lift and Microlift
	Trubos Lifts	Industrial service and goods lifts

High level of specification

Permanent adjustable dock leveller – mechanical or hydraulic – built into loading platform.	Becker Lifts	Range of Serco levellers
	Evans Lifts	Range of Hunter levellers
	Gascoigne Engineering	Range of dock levellers
	Hafa	Range of dock levellers
	Hi-Lo	Modular Take Away Loading Bays and permanent dock levellers
	Leiston Engineering	Range of Topper levellers
	Power Loading	Range of dock levellers
	Stokvis	Range of Kelley levellers
Self-contained electric traction or hydraulic-type lift with self-supporting metal framework and a solid, possibly weatherproof, enclosure.	Barron & Shepherd	Range of goods lifts
	Becker Lifts	Range of goods lifts
	Evans Lifts	Range of goods lifts
	Gough & Co	Range of goods lifts
	Oakland Elevators	Range of goods lifts
Loading bay shelter of tear resistant material; caters for varying vehicle heights and widths.	Eriks-Allied	Range of dock shelters
	Evans Lifts	Range of Hunter shelters and seals
	Hafa	Range of dock shelters
	Hi-Lo	Range of dock shelters
	Leiston Engineering	Range of Topper shelters and seals
	Stokvis	Range of Frommelt shelters
	Stowaway	Airlink inflatable dock seal
	Trelleborg	Tretight seals

External elements

Prefabricated units used to provide shelter or storage; also units to store refuse for disposal. The provision of external elements – storage, waste disposal, etc – is often an afterthought, but for both practical and aesthetic reasons consideration should be given to them at an early stage in the planning process. To help decide on elements and level of specification the following should be considered/determined:

Basic considerations

— What are external shelters of storage units required for? Shelter for cars or bicycles; storage of gas cylinders or flammable liquids or toxic, corrosive and other dangerous materials, etc?
— Are the shelters or storage units intended to be temporary or permanent?
— What types of refuse will have to be disposed of? What forms of storage containers

or other equipment will be required for handling the refuse?
— Consider how and by whom the refuse will be removed from the premises. How regularly will this be done?
— Determine how building and/or fire regulations will affect the proposed provision. What other controls are there, e.g. approval of building owner?

Shelters and stores

— Should shelters be instantly removable – e.g. lightweight steel frame with plastic cover and, possibly, fold away – or of a more permanent type of construction?
— Are there any special requirements for shelters, e.g. extent of enclosure (roof only or roof and one side, etc); cycle stands which form part of supporting framework, etc?
— Storage units: the type of material to be stored and the degree of security needed will

influence the choice in terms of materials and construction. Units may, for example, be of pre-cast concrete, metal or timber.

— Where will the unit stand? Will a foundation or base be required?

— Consider what type of supports would be most suitable, e.g. legs, skids, wheels or concrete base.

— Is it important for supports to be adjustable, e.g. hydraulic jacklegs?

— Consider type and position of door, windows, grills, etc.

— Is there a possibility that the unit may need to be extended at some later date?

Refuse disposal

— What is the nature and quantity of the refuse to be disposed of? Must any of the refuse be stored separately, e.g. high grade waste paper (from computers, for example)?

— Determine the volume of different types of waste that storage must be provided for.

— Waste materials are visually unattractive; consider how and where they can be stored until removal. Are there any special precautions that need to be taken, e.g. flammable or toxic wastes?

— If waste is bulky and low density consider using waste compactor – material is compressed and retained for disposal in closed containers. This method may not only save space and transportation costs but also reduce

fire risk of stored refuse.

Construction

— Are units under consideration sturdily constructed? Vandal resistant? Non-combustible?

— Are components (walls, floor, roof) adequately insulated?

— Can units be easily extended? Can they be readily moved/relocated with the use of a crane or other special equipment.

— Will lighting or other services be required? Is unit supplied ready to plug into required mains services?

Appearance and maintenance

— Consider the appearance of the unit; will it be compatible with the immediate surroundings, e.g. adjacent buildings, landscape elements, etc?

— Are all surfaces and details durable and weatherproof? Can they be easily cleaned and maintained?

— What internal finishes are supplied as standard?

Cost

— Compare the installation, maintenance and in-use costs for the units under consideration.

Table 31 External elements. Levels of specification and manufacturers.

Basic level of specification	Suppliers and manufacturers	
External shelter: steel frame with roof covering and possibly with cladding on one or more sides; alternatively, steel frame with plastic cover, usually fold away.	Abix (Metal Industries) Ltd	Range of shelters and cycle stands
	C & A Canopies	Range of standard canopies
	Odoni	Range of shelters and cycle stands
	Rutland Products	Up 'n' Over car cover
	Welconstruct	Shelters and cycle racks
Simple containers either to screen dustbins or house paper or plastic refuse sacks.	Dartford Metalcrofts	Rotary sack holders
	Hardall	Mobile refuse containers
	Marley Buildings	Sack Tidy
	Reed Medway	Range of sack holders
	Reinforced Concrete	RCC Concrete Dustbin Stores
Medium level of specification		
External store: prefabricated units in element or volumetric form. Not necessarily fireproof.	Bullock & Driffill	Bulpax Moovabouts
	C & R Constructions	Mobipac and Mobilspace Expandapac units
	Elliotts of Peterborough	Spaceway units
	Glasdon	Olympic modular GRP units
	Swiftplan	Rapidplan units
	Redispace	Portable Stores
	Reinforced Concrete Construction	RCC Concrete Stores

Steel self-tipping skips on base frame fitted for fork lift truck use and with castors if required.	Down & Francis	Range of self-tipping hoppers
	Key Industrial Equipment	Range of self-tipping skips
	Thetford Compactors	Tipa skips and enclosed containers

High level of specification

External store: prefabricated unit in element or volumetric form. High security and fireproof. Wide range off fitting out options.	Anmac	Range of GRC Cabins
	Cosalt Adda Systems	Adda Space units
	Masterplan	Portable units and security stores
	Marley Buildings	Flamestor
	Panelite	Super Stores
	Portasilo	Portastor range of security units
	Powys Buildings	Pegasus portable units
	Presco Buildings	Steelclad units, also Safestore and Superstore units
	Swiftplan	Spacejac units
	Terrapin	Range of steel store units
	Torton Budies	Nomad Mobiles
	Trausline	Transguard steel security units
	Rilocatable Accommodation	Range of temporary units
	Wyseplan	Monostore
	Youngman	Rovacabin S units
Compactor unit with closed container for waste storage while awaiting removal and disposal.	Dartford Metalcrafts	London refuse compactor systems
	Hardall	Refuse compactors
	Reed Medway	Range of compactors
	Thetford Compactors	Range of compactor equipment
	Waste Compaction Systems	Refupak

INDEPENDENT SERVICES

Security

Devices and/or equipment to protect space, property and confidential material against premeditated crime.
Security should, generally speaking, be regarded as a system made up of various components. Consideration of solutions during the design stage is essential – rather than waiting until the building is in use – but it must be realised that no system will be 100% secure. It can, however, be regarded as successful if it delays entry and, in so doing, deters the intruder or exposes him to detection and possible apprehension. To help decide on the appropriate system and level of specification the following must be considered/determined:

Basic requirements

— What are the overall objectives? What is the security system required to do? What areas need special protection? What will be contained in those areas – confidential information, money, valuable equipment, etc?

— Will the premises need special forms of security not only when unoccupied but also during working hours?
— Does the insurance company have any specific requirements? What reduction in premiums could be expected?

Detection systems and alarms

— There are various forms of detection systems; only the basic types are described in broad outline.
• Continuous wiring stretched across an opening; activated by cutting or displacement.
• Metallic foil applied in strips to glass; activated when glass is broken or when strips are removed.
• Protective switch fitted into frame of door or window; activated when door or window is opened more than 100 mm.
• Pressure mats concealed under carpets in strategic positions.
• Rigid panels or boards covered with printed circuit wiring; used to protect smaller areas, e.g. safes.
• Vibration detectors fitted to glass or in roof space, etc.

• Volumetric detectors, i.e. devices activated by movement within space or by heat/electrical capacity given off by person entering space. Various types, e.g. microwave, ultrasonic, infra-red, etc.

• Acoustic devices programmed to react to certain types of sound.

— Detectors are linked to alarms; consider which type will be most suitable:

• Audible alarm, e.g. bells.

• 'Silent' (not heard by intruder), e.g. flashing lights or machine which either dials 999 and relays pre-recorded message or contacts control centre of alarm company, who inform police. Detectors can be connected to central control unit – micro-processor type can be programmed to respond in various ways, e.g. sounding alarms; signalling the police, etc. Fire detectors can be linked to the same control unit.

Windows and doors

— Windows and doors are, obviously, the most common means of illegal entry into a building. How accessible are they? Are they in exposed or concealed positions?

— How secure are the fastening/locking devices on doors and opening windows?

— How securely are the frames fixed to the surrounding walls?

— Are doors of solid construction? Are windows double glazed?

— Before deciding on detection devices consider whether bars, grilles and/or security shutters would provide an adequate degree of protection.

Roofs and roof openings

• How accessible is the roof from the ground, neighbouring buildings, climbable pipes or escape straits?

• How vulnerable is the roof construction to forced entry? Can covering (tiles, sheets, etc) be easily removed?

• Are there any roof openings such as doors or rooflights? Consider their location in terms of ease of access, roof pitch and degree of exposure or concealment.

• How secure are the fastening/locking devices, and the frames or kerbs?

• Before deciding on detection devices, consider whether bars or grilles (fitted below rooflight kerbs for example) would provide an adequate degree of protection.

Other components

— Will special storage be required for smaller valuable items – cash, equipment, documents, confidential research, etc? If so, consider the installation of a safe or strongroom; specialist advice should be obtained.

— Consider need for shredder(s). May be essential in duplicating room if confidential reports are produced regularly.

— Will it be important to control access to the premises or to special areas of risk? Doors to premises and/or restricted area may be fitted with identification device (e.g. coded cards) or remotely controlled electric locks. The simplest way of keeping track of who is in the building at any given time is by ensuring that all staff and visitors sign or clock in and out.

General considerations

— A basic problem with many detector/alarm systems is their tendency to be set off accidentally. Consider balance between sensitivity and reliability of the different methods.

— Consider problem of cleaners moving through the premises during times when the building is otherwise unoccupied.

Cost

— Compare installation, maintenance and in-use costs for the systems/equipment under consideration.

Table 32 Security. Levels of specification and manufacturers.

Basic level of specification	Suppliers and manufacturers	
Perimeter detectors/alarms – continuous wiring, metallic foil, protective switches, etc – fitted to external doors, windows and rooflights. With audible alarm.	AFA Minerva	Perimeter detection systems
	ELS	Door alarms
	Lloyds Security	Perimeter detection systems
	Mather & Platt	Door, window and shutter alarms
Medium level of specification		
Perimeter detectors as for basic but with device for contacting police or control centre of alarm company.	See basic levels, above	
Shredding machine.	Bankers Box	Intershred range
	Business Aids	Web range

	Ofrex	Fordigraph range
	Ofshred	Range of shredding machines
	Portable Factory Equipment	Range of shredding machines
	Reed Medway	Range of shredding machines
	Rexel	Versishred range
Clocking-in equipment at main entrance(s).	Blick International	Time/flexitime recorders
	Reliance Systems	Clock and time recorder systems
	Tann-Synchronome	Time/flexitime recorders

High level of specification

Systems of internal detector devices, e.g. pressure mats and/or volumetric detectors with compatible perimeter detectors. Detectors linked to device for contacting police or control centre of alarm company, possibly via microprocessor control unit (see also Fire Protection, p.66).	AFA Minerva	Various systems
	Carters	Range of space detection systems
	Lloyds Security	Various systems
	Mather & Platt	Security systems
	Reliance	Ghost Security System (sound detection)
	Static Systems Group	Statiscan security monitoring and control systems
	STC Electronic	Intruder alarm systems
	Zetter	Intruder alarm systems
Access control to entrance(s) or area of special risk.	BSG	Corkey and other access/control systems
	ELS	Digican and card access systems
	Group 4	Securimaster
	RSS Group	Cardscan access control system
	STC Electronic	Access control systems
	Tann Cardentry	Access control system
Safe or strongroom.	BSG	Range of wall safes
	Chubb	Range of safes including underfloor type
	ELS	Range of wall safes
	Security	Protector range of underfloor safes
	Welconstruct	Various ranges of safes

Communications systems

Equipment for direct external and internal communication – verbal, written or drawn. Effective communications – appropriate for the scale and type of operation – are important to all organisations. Cable ducts and/or trunking must be provided, so the system to be used should be decided upon at an early stage. Advice may be obtained from the Telephone Area Manager. Before deciding on the appropriate system and level of specification the following must be considered/determined:

Basic requirements

— What are the needs of the organisation? What is the frequency of telephone use, i.e. incoming and outgoing calls? Is internal

telephone communication important and, if so, how frequently is it likely to be used?
— Any decision on the type of system will depend on number of staff, layout of office and likelihood of expansion. As charges for connection and alteration are high it may be advisable to overestimate slightly for the initial installation.
— Will any special equipment or systems be needed? (See following paragraph.)

Telephone systems

Consider which of the following basic systems will be most appropriate:
— Simple installations for small offices, consisting of one or more exchange lines each connected to a telephone instrument. If more phones are required – up to 10 – Keymasters

(supplied by BT) may be used, i.e. one or two master instruments on the exchange line, each with up to 5 extensions. Incoming calls may be received by one of the extensions if required or transferred to any of them from the master instrument. Internal communication is also possible.
— Larger installations require a switchboard with an operator or supervisor. There are two basic types:

• Private Manual Branch Exchange (PMBX), which enables the provision of a selected number of extensions. Incoming and outgoing calls as well as internal communication must all be made via the switchboard and handled by the operator. This system is suitable for offices with a relatively low frequency of calls and little or no need for internal telephone communications.
• Private Automatic Branch Exchange (PABX). Various types are available. The PABX 1 is most commonly used and can accommodate up to 10 exchange lines and 49 internal extensions. All the types allow outgoing and inter-extension calls to be made without involving the operator, i.e. an outgoing line is usually obtained by dialling 9 and extensions can be dialled by number. This system should only be considered if frequency of both internal and external use will be heavy.
— Computerised systems are available which contain an automatic call record feature, i.e. the extension number of the caller, the time and duration of the call, etc, are all recorded for subsequent printout.
— If external traffic is very heavy it may be advisable to have a separate system for internal communications. Various additional services – fire alarms, call systems, etc – can be incorporated. The following basic types may be considered:
• Push-button type (from BT or private manufacturer): can give links with up to 16 phones, but if there are more than 6 the installation tends to become rather clumsy. Disadvantages: the heavy cables required and the lack of privacy – conversations may be overheard from other extensions.
• Private Automatic Exchange (PAX). From private manufacturer. Extensions are dialled through an unmanned exchange.

• An alternative is an intercom system, the disadvantage being that there is no privacy, but it can be used to pass general messages and to locate staff.

Special telephone instruments/apparatus

Consider whether any of the following will be either useful or essential:
— Loudspeaking phones which allow both hands to be kept free: various models available with loudspeakers and microphones in combined or separate units.
— Callmakers which store telephone numbers and dial selected ones when activated. Card type uses punched cards to call number and has unlimited capacity. Tape type stores up to 400 numbers on magnetic tape. There are various other systems available.
— Answering sets which can be used when office is closed or switchboard is unmanned. They are connected to telephone and when activated by incoming call, they transmit pre-recorded message and record message from caller. Can be used to record important telephone conversation.
— Transmission of facsimiles by feeding document (text or graphic) into an electronic machine which can be purchased or rented. Alternative is instrument with special pad, on which messages are written or drawn, which is connected to the telephone.
— Datel service for organisations employing computer processes: provides instant access through the telephone network to automated information systems.

Telex

— Telex – basically a teleprinter – allows typewritten material to be transmitted to any other telex user anywhere in the world. This is worth considering when rapid, accurate response is required frequently.

Cost

— Compare the installation, maintenance and in-use costs for the systems under consideration.

Table 33 Communications systems. Levels of specification and manufacturers.

Basic level of specification	Suppliers and manufacturers	
One telephone unit per 40 m². If more than two telephones are required one Keymaster for up to five extensions or two Keymasters for up to ten extensions. (Alternative use of common switchboard shared with other building tenants.)	British Telecom	Keymaster systems
Intercom system for relaying general messages and to locate staff.	Barkway Electronics	Polydex intercom systems
	Blick	Intercom systems
	Cass Electronics	Ringmaster intercom
	Fonadek	GE-168 wireless intercom
	Haos	Nutone IMA-516 Commu-ni-Com
	Panasonic	National intercom systems
	Plessey	Intercom Systems
	Pye Business Systems	Philips M100 intercom system
	Rediffusion	Intercom Systems
	Shipton	Intercom Systems
	Thorn Ericsson	Ericom system
	Transcall	Translink system
	Truesound	Intercom system
Medium level of specification		
One telephone unit per 30 m². Possible installation of PMBX.	British Telecom	PMBX systems
Internal telephones: push-button type.	Blick	Sprint push button and Exes 5000 systems
	British Telecom	Internal telephone systems
	Panasonic	National push-button system
	Shipton	Internal telephone systems
	Thorn Ericsson	Ericom system
	Transcall	Push-button system
Special equipment: callmaker and/or answering set.	Ansamatic	Telephone answering systems
	British Telecom	Callmakers and Answering Sets
	Code-A-Phone	Answering machines, electronic diallers, etc
	Dictaphone	Dictacall answering machine
	Feedback	Answering machines
	Geemark	Ansamac answering machines
	GMT	Answering equipment
	GTE	Answer phones
	Panasonic	National answering machines
	Shipton	Answering machines

High level of specification		
One telephone unit per 20 m^2. Possible installation of PABX – may be computerised system.	British Telecom	PABX systems
	IBM	1750 and 3750 systems
	International Computers	DNX-2000 digital private exchange
	ITT Business Systems	Unimat 4080 modular computerised exchange and other systems
	Mitel Telecom	Superswitch system
	Planned Equipment	Electronic PABX system
	Plessey	PDX system
	Pye Business Systems	EBX and PABX systems
	Reliance Systems	SL1 electronic systems
	Siemens	PABX systems
	Telephone Rentals	PDX computer based exchange
	Thorn Ericsson	PABX systems and Diavox 824 systems
Internal telephones: PAX systems.	Blick	Modernphone system
	Cass Electronics	PAX systems
	ITT Business Systems	Internal communications system
	Panasonic	National system
	Planned Equipment	Electronic PAX system
	Plessey	Paxtel system
	Pye Business Systems	UPX systems
	Siemens	PAX Systems
	Trident	Electronic PAX system
Special facilities: telex and/or facsimile transmission, and/or Datel.	3M	Range of facsimile transmission equipment
	British Telecom	Telex and Datel
	Chernikeeff	Autex 1600 telex
	CSL Business Systems	System 4000 telex
	Delpha Systems	Data Transfer 1020 Series (telex)
	Interscan	Dexnet facsimile transmission
	ITT Business Systems	Telefax facsimile transceivers and telex equipment
	Panasonic	UF-520EX facsimile transceiver
	Plessey	Fax facsimile transmission
	Rank Xerox	Range of facsimile transmission equipment
	Shipton	Facsimile transmission equipment
	Siemens	Teleprinters and facsimile transmission equipment
	Transtel	Telex equipment
	Trend	Telex equipment

FURNITURE, FITTINGS AND ACCESSORIES

Furniture: office systems

Desks, chairs, workplace storage, display units, etc, supplied either individually or as elements of a co-ordinated range.

Furniture and screening (see also p.80) must be selected and positioned with care to ensure that it suits operational needs and the specific space in question. The appearance and quality will also have a major influence on the corporate image which is projected and on the satisfaction of the employees. To help decide on the appropriate furniture system and level of specification the following must be considered/determined:

Basic strategy

— What type of workplaces are to be provided, e.g. in individual offices or open-plan/landscaped space? If open-plan space is being used, what work method is used and how are workplaces to be organised, e.g. independent, clustered or ganged (linked in continuous lines)? Are the places to be enclosed or not?

— Consider the overall quality and appearance required. Remember that furniture and screening can affect the sense of space and the image, or general impression, considerably.

— What type of furniture system will be most appropriate for the defined needs? Furniture systems are generally classified as follows:

● Independent elements usually in a range of separate items which match in terms of design, construction and finish.
● Co-ordinated components which may be used individually or combined to form a variety of workplace types.
● Panel-hung systems: self-supporting screens – which may accept clip-on lights as well as power and telephone points – which in turn support various separate elements, i.e. desks, bookshelves, storage units, etc.
● Combinations of panel-hung and coordinated components.

Flexibility

— Is flexibility of workstation layouts a priority? How many different types of workstations are needed? Consider whether the systems under consideration can meet the requirements, i.e. satisfy all work-functional needs for all levels of staff.

— Can the individual components be easily assembled, demounted and moved without special help? Can components not in use be easily and compactly stored?

— Will it be easy to obtain separate components at a later date should the need for expansion or replacement arise?

— Will the system function in both open-plan and cellular office spaces?

Components: requirements

— Consider specific workstation requirements for each individual or group:
● Desks: sizes and heights for various uses. Will desks be independent units – possibly with side tables – or will they be linked to form clustered or ganged workstations? What additional elements are required, e.g. pedestals with drawers and/or lockable unit, modesty panels, etc? Will special V D U terminal furniture be required?
● Chairs: sizes and heights of seats and backrests to ensure correct posture and support for specific task. Must chairs have arms? Adjustable seats and arms? Swivel and tilt actions? Pedestals with plastic slides or castors?
● Storage provision adjoining desks: what must be stored – range, quantity, sizes and weights? Must units be low or high level? Fixed or mobile? Shelves, drawers, cupboards and/or filing system?
● Display: blackboards, pinboards.
● Screening: will screens have integrated services or not? Must concealed wiring be able to run horizontally as well as vertically? Two basic methods are used, i.e. 'lay-in' – a channel with cover plate – and surface mounted 'clip-on' cable. Make sure system is simple and accessible both in screens and furniture units which form part of wire management system.

Construction

— How robust is the construction? Will construction and materials used be able to withstand normal wear and tear, and support the weight of persons, equipment and machines?

— Are all units rigid when assembled and free from vibration during use, e.g. typing?

— Do moving parts – drawers, castors, etc – operate quietly and smoothly?

— Consider possible hazards: projecting legs, sharp edges or corners, etc.

Finish and maintenance

— Consider overall appearance in terms of image/effect required and compatibility with interior design concept.

— What finishes, textures, colours would be most suitable for work surfaces, upholstery, legs, etc? Are all surfaces suitable for function (work surfaces non-reflective) and can they be easily cleaned, maintained and, if necessary, replaced? Will they chip or scratch easily?

— Does layout and system of construction allow for easy floor cleaning?

Cost

— Compare the installation, maintenance and in-use costs for the systems under consideration.

Table 34 Furniture; office systems. Levels of specification and manufacturers.

Basic level of specification	Suppliers and manufacturers	
Independent units – desks, chairs, storage cupboard, etc – which may be part of matching range.	Abbott Bros	Abbess range
	Allard & Co	Range of office furniture
	BMG	Modular range
	Caplan Profile Group	Range of office furniture
	Carson	400 Group range
	City Contract	Mentor range
	Continental Comfort	King Classic II range
	Alan Cooper	Range of office furniture
	Dan Off Nordia	Nipu range
	Desking Systems	Oxford range
	Dodson Bull Interiors	Artifort range
	Ergonom Distributors	Range of office furniture
	ESA	6000 Series range
	Faran	Alfa and other ranges
	Flexiform	Flexiburo range
	Giroflex	Range of seating
	G. A. Harvey	Range of office furniture
	Hille	Range of office furniture
	Isoplan	Range of office furniture
	Kartel Division (WCB)	Kartell range
	Key Industrial	Range of office furniture
	Linden Pride	Kinnarps range
	Matthews	Range of office furniture
	Herman Miller	Range of office furniture
	Mines & West	Utopia range
	A. Murray	Team Line, Tenani and other ranges
	OMK Design	Range of office furniture
	Project Office Furniture	Range of office furniture
	Quatrefoil Design	Quatrefoil range
	Ramchester	Range of office furniture
	Gordon Russell	Series 90 range of office furniture
	Sankey Sheldon	Euroform range
	Scott Howard	Range of office furniture
	Shannon	VDU furniture range
	Sintocel	Range of office furniture
	Tan-Sad	Compact 1000 and 2000 ranges
	Twinlock	Ashdown and Dunmere ranges
	Voko	Range of office furniture
	Welcon struct	Range of office furniture
	Western Trading	Range of office furniture
	Wiltshier	All Steel range
	Windsor Enterprises	Onda range
Medium level of specification		
Coordinated range of desks, chairs, storage and screens with limited accessories.	Apton	IP 20 system
	Capton Profile Group	Narus 2 range
	Communications	CCD communications workstation furniture
	Complex Design	
	Dan Off	Nipu Room Line screen based system
	Dodson Bull Interiors	Ahrend range
	Ergonom Distributors	Misura furniture range
	Facit Furniture	Data and Ekonom range
	Faram	Sistema ABC
	Form International	Stephens System
	GCF	Various ranges
	Hartland Bentheim	Olivetti Synthesis ranges

	Grant Westfield	KI Cumulus range
	Heals Contracts	Onda system
	Hopkins Green	Arbor system
	Integrated Furniture	Mauser range
	Intercraft	Epsilon range
	Interspace	Castelli range
	Kerrison Furnishing	Marcadet Series 9000 range
	Kewlox Furniture	Driad system
	Lucas Furniture	Programme 1 system
	Martela	Conti range
	Medfurn Interiors	Univer and Discovery systems
	Herman Miller	Burdick Group system
	Mines & West	Utopia VDU workstations and Bieffe range
	Office & Electronic Machines	Van Berks Optiforma system
	Office Contracts	Trio Moduli range
	Office Trends	Trend range
	Orga-Tech	Ergodata system
	Malcolm Owen	Quorum, Datatec and Trident ranges
	Plumb Contracts	Catch 4 and Fantoni ranges
	William Plunket	Highline system (combined with Screenform screens)
	SMP	Educat system
	Unit 4	TM52 and TM53 ranges
	Wiltshier	All Steel range

High level of specification

Coordinated range of linked and/or panel-hung components – desk, chairs, storage, screens, etc – including wire management and task lighting.	Allard & Co	3K Compart and Integra M200 system
	Amseco	Furniture system
	Aram Designs	Arflex system
	Arenson International	Genesis system
	Beam Office Equipment	Gesika system
	Carson	Link 900
	City Contract	Sistema Aster 22
	Click Systems	Click system
	Continental Comfort	King Delta 2 system
	Alan Cooper	Framac or Contour ranges with System Screens
	DP Office Concepts	Five Plus system
	Ergonom Distributors	Modulo 3 system with Misura screen system
	Faram	Superalfa system
	Facit Furniture	Facit 80 system
	Flexiform	Kasparian BKD system
	Form International	Stephens system
	Grant International	Gispen TP system
	G.A. Harvey	System One
	Hille	HOS/80 System
	Homeworks	Karl Hayes furniture and panel system
	Hopkins Green	System B8 Series 800
	Integrated Furniture	Mauser V2R system
	Intercraft	Transform 2 system
	Isoplan	Isoplan system
	John Lewis	Plansystem
	Kerrison Furnishing	Option system

Lucas Furniture	Programme 2 system
Matthews	MD System and Amseco system
Martela	In Team system
Herman Miller	Action Office
Martin Neil Designs	Nobo system
NKR	NKR Pro system
OMK Design	OMK Office
Plumb Contracts	PSO system
Project Office Furniture	4000 Range plus screens
Sankey Sheldon	System 2000
Scott Howard	Castelli Pert and Haller systems
Sisk	Series 3 system
Steelcase Strafor	Steelcase Strafor 9000 and 400 system
Swedeline	Round office and Koppla systems
Tan-Sad	Unitan system
Unit 4	TM BOX system
Vickers	System E combined with RMF range
Voko	MEP/R 30 system
Westinghouse	ASD + system
Wilkinson Proteus	Proteus system
Wiltshier	9000 range and All Steel 8000 system

Office storage

Equipment for the storage and retrievel of information, stationery and supplies, but excluding individual storage, which is part of the workstation (see Furniture: office systems, p.98). Storage tends to be a neglected part of office planning. The storage and retrieval of increasing amounts of information – a problem which most organisations are confronted with – is extremely important and the provision of equipment to ensure that this is efficiently done requires careful assessment. To help decide on the appropriate system and level of specification the following must be considered/determined:

Basic requirements

—   Before considering the hardware which will be required the following questions must be answered:

●   What must be stored? For example: information and confidential documents – files, computer software, printouts and punch cards, microfilm, photographs, drawings, literature and catalogues; stationery and office supplies; special equipment – typewriters, calculators, surveying instruments, etc. Draw up an inventory.
●   How much of each type of material will need storage space? How much space will it occupy? How heavy will it be? Where should it be kept?
●   How often will it be used and what speed of access will be required?
●   How long must the various categories of material be kept? What proportion of storage must be short term/current, and long term/bulk?
—   Objectives must be defined and techniques to be used (indexing, equipment and housing, etc) investigated.

Flexibility

—   What degree of flexibility will be required? When assessing equipment/systems consider how flexibly they can be used (i.e. range of material which can be stored) and how easily they can be altered and added to. Will it be easy to obtain additional units at a later date?
—   If equipment is not part of office furniture system how compatible is it in design?
—   Will the system function equally well in both cellular and open-plan office spaces and, if necessary, in special storage areas?

Types of equipment

—   Consider the types of equipment in terms of defined objectives and the material to be stored:

●   Adjustable shelving of timber and/or metal cantilevered or framed supports – for stationery, literature and catalogues, bulk storage, etc.
●   Tote boxes of plastic with open ends in a range of sizes and colours – flexible storage for small items (stationery, drawing supplies, samples, etc). Can be stacked or mounted in special units, e.g. trolley base, wall panel or cabinet.
●   Filing cabinet (drawer type) of metal which can be lockable and fireproof – for storage of current files.

• Rotary filing system with circular shelves or trays supported on central revolving pillar. Can be freestanding or enclosed in cabinet which may be lockable and fireproof. Not always very flexible as the manufacturer's own cards, files, boxes, etc, may have to be used. Capacity and accessibility is good.

• Lateral filing cabinets are available in a variety of proprietary types. They are more flexible and adaptable than drawer type filing cabinets and have a range of interchangeable components. May be open fronted or fitted with roller shutters or doors. For storage of files, computer software, cassettes, microfilm, etc.

• Mobile units allow high concentration of storage. Units are usually fitted with wheels running on tracks and may move from side to side or forwards, and backwards.

• Storage units for drawings, plans (A2–A1 size); either horizontal, in cabinets with drawers, or vertical with drawings held on suspension strips or in folders. Various proprietary systems available.

Construction and finish

— How robust is the construction? Are all units rigid when assembled and will they be able to support the required load?

— Do moving parts – drawers, slides, castors, etc – operate quietly and smoothly?

— What finishes and colours are available? Consider overall appearance and compatibility with other furnishings.

General considerations

— Security: for confidential files and important documents. Are lockable, fire resistant cabinets adequate or will a safe be required? (See also Security, p.92).

— Protection from dust: what material must be stored behind doors or blinds, or in drawers?

— Heights of storage units: if tall units are to be provided will they be for long term storage only? Consider accessibility of material stored at higher level.

Cost

Compare the installation, maintenance and in-use costs for the systems under consideration.

Table 35 Office storage. Levels of specification and manufacturers.

Basic level of specification	Suppliers and manufacturers	
Shelving of softwood or metal. Cantilevered or frame construction. Low height, few accessories.	Arenson International	President modular shelving
	Bankers Box	Shelving and bin units
	Bruynzeil Storage Systems	Shelving
	Cube Store	Cube Shelf
	Dexion	Slotted Angle system
	Ensiform Type Products	Raaco shelving
	ESA	5000 Series
	Grant International	Gispen Regale shelving
	James Hill	Shelving
	Link 51	Handy Tube and Clip-on systems
	Matthews Office Furniture	Shelving systems
	Office & Electronic Machines	Van Blerk Optiforma archive and beam racks
	Quatrefoil	Shelving
	Remploy	Lundia systems
	Sherwood Steel	Shelving and bin units
	Sintacel	Top Track shelving
	Tebrax	Shelving system
	United Storage	Shelving and bin units
	Welconstruct	Slotted steel shelving
Stackable totes (bins)/trays of coloured plastic for flexible storage of stationery and small items.	Bankers Box	Stax on Steel and High-Stak, etc.
	Esselte Dymo	Sorty sorting and storage trays
	Expandex	Interstak (stackable corrugated-board drawer units)
	James Hill	Small parts containers
	Key Industrial	Top range of polypropylene bins

Steel filing cabinets, four-drawer, lockable and fireproof.	Arenson International	President modular filing
	Bankers Box	Filing cabinet range
	Grant International	Gispen cabinets
	Harvey Office Furniture	Card and document filing cabinets
	Key International Equipment	Filing cabinet range
	Matthews Office Furniture	Filing cabinet range
	Sankey Sheldon	Filing cabinet range
	TBS	Filing cabinet range
	Welconstruct	Filing cabinet range
	Peter Williams	Filing cabinet range
	Willis Computer Supplies	Filing cabinet range

Medium level of specification

Metal shelving systems, low or high rise with wide range of accessories.	Cube Store	Cubekit storage and shelving system
	Dexion	Impex 38 system
	Key Industrial Equipment	Filing and office shelving system
	Welconstruct	WSM system
	Herbert Zippel	Accommodator range
Plastic totes/trays (as for Basic, above) but with support units, e.g. shelving, cupboards or racks.	Dexion	Maxi small-part storage used with Impex
	Esselte Dymo	Sorty system
	Key Industrial Equipment	Keytop racks and trolleys with Top bins
	Sintacel	Mobile Storage and Shelfa Bulk Storage Units
Rotary filing cabinets.	Elite Manufacturing	Rotary filing systems
	Key Industrial Equipment	Rotalite
	Matthews Office Furniture	Roundabout
	Railex Systems	Railex Rotary
	Rotadex Systems	Platfile
	Templestock	Rota-Trieve circular filing cabinet

High level of specification

Lateral cabinet system with wide range of dividers. Alternatively, complete system of storage walls.	Acco	Accodata storage system
	Arenson International	President filing furniture
	Arrange Marketing	Holzapfel Interwall flexible system of storage walls
	Alan Bedford Ltd	Behr 1634 system
	Bruynzeel Storage Systems	Office storage and filing systems
	Bankers Box	Stax-Tab lateral filing
	Caplan Profile Group	Storflex system
	Carson	Range of storage units
	Carter-Parrat Group	DP documentation filing system
	Cave & Tab	Tab storage system
	City Contract	Range of storage systems
	Alan Cooper	Framac System
	Don Off Nordia	Nipu storage cabinets
	Dexion	Plan-D storage and filing system (static or mobile)

	DP Office Concepts	Design Plus storage system
	Elite Manufacturing	Lateral storage system
	Ergonom Distributors	Misura storage units
	Esselte Dymo	Pendaflex filing system
	Faram	Progetto 450 storage wall and filing system
	Factory & Office Equipment	Top storage and filing system
	Flexi Form	Flexiburo System
	Fonadek International	Styro storage and filing system
	Grant International	Gispen Programme
	G. A. Harvey	Harvey range of storage units
	Intercraft	Intercraft System
	Kardex Systems	Kardex storage and filing system
	Kerrison Furnishing	Marcadet storage and filing units
	Key Industrial Equipment	Storage and filing systems
	Lucas Furniture	Programme storage and filing system
	Matthews Office Furniture	Matthews storage and filing system
	Martin Neil Designs	Fairfield range of storage units
	Medfurn Interiors	Discovery storage walls
	Office & Electronic Machines	Van Blerk Optiforma system cabinets
	Orga-Tech	Storage Units
	Project Interiors	Varistat storage wall system
	Project Office Furniture	5000 Range and 9000 Range High Density systems
	Railex Systems	Range of filing furniture
	Royal Sovereign	Filing systems
	Sankey Sheldon	Varimaster System
	Shannon	Storage and filing system
	Steelcase Strafor	MR 400 System
	TBS	Triumph Omni-file system
	Twinlock	Storage and filing system
	United Storage	Lateral filing units
	Vickers Furniture	System E
	Voko	Section storage units
	Peter Williams	Vertilec and Slimstack systems
	Willis Computer Supplies	Storage and filing system
	Herbert Zippel	Storage and filing system
Special storage units, e.g. plan storage, special computer software storage, etc.	DP Office Concepts	Vertical hanging files, etc.
	Matthews Office Furniture	Vertical cabinets, computer storage, etc.
	Vistaplan	Viscount cabinet
	Western Trading	Westra computer storage
	Willis Computer Supplies	Computer storage
	Wiltshier Contract Furnishing	All Steel Storex system
	Herbert Zippel	Zippel plan filing

Special furniture and fittings

For entrance/reception areas, meeting – or boardrooms and display/demonstration areas. The spaces in question will be regularly used by clients/customers and visitors and should, therefore, not only set the tone of the workplace in terms of appearance, atmosphere and efficiency, but also have a major influence on the corporate image which is projected. To help decide on the furniture, fittings and level of specification the following must be considered/determined:

Entrance/reception

— How is premises approached? Remember entry begins on street or public lobby/passage. Consider firm's nameplate and directional signs (see Signage, p.114), letter-box, etc.
— Will external door be kept locked? If so, consider a two-way loudspeaker/intercom (or telephone entry) system with electric door-opening mechanism.
— What will the function of the reception area be? Simple boundary between entrance and open arrangement beyond; linked with switchboard or secretarial space; contain waiting area with seating and/or display area.
— What furniture will be required? Reception desk, high counter, enquiry hatch; seating – individual chairs or modular units – table for reading matter, ashtray, etc; stand or hooks for overcoats, hats and umbrellas; display fittings (see below).

Meeting room or boardroom

— Will this be a separate room or part of another space (e.g. executive office) which may be divided by a movable partition (see p.48).
— What will the room be used for? Meetings and seminars; presentations including projection of films, video, slides, etc; entertainment; interviews, etc.
— What size and shape of table will best suit the available space and the functions for which it will be used? If mainly for formal meetings rectangular shape may be best; alternative shapes – for example, circular or horseshoe – could be better for less formal use. If flexibility – various arrangements for different uses – is important, consider tables which are built up out of separate sections.
— Chairs need to be comfortable, of durable construction and materials, and not too heavy, as they must be easily moved.
— What display and/or storage units will be required, e.g. photographs, products, brochures; books, projectors and other equipment, drinks and glassware, etc?
— What fittings will be needed for presentation equipment, e.g. separate table for projectors?

— Is there sufficient wall space for the required presentation aids, e.g. pinboards, writing boards, projection screens, wall charts etc?

Presentation aids

— Which type of writing-board will be most suitable, e.g. chalkboard (green or black) or whiteboard either for use with water based felt tipped pens or dry marker pens? All are available with surfaces that can take magnetic symbols and letters.
— Boards may be freestanding or wall hung; single panel or with fixed back panels and sliding or folding front panels; of one material only or any combination of the following: chalkboard, whiteboard, pinboard and projection screens.
— What type of projection screen will be needed, e.g. for standard projection only or for both overhead and standard projection? The screen may need to be adjustable to give suitable angle for overhead projection. Consider size, also whether retractable, fixed to part, or part of, writing-board.
— Will any visual planning system be required? A wide range of methods (pegboard, slotted board, channelled board, T-card, bar chart, etc) and if types (leave planners, progress planners, statistic planners, computer loading charts, etc) are available. Be sure that the correct system for individual requirements is chosen; advice may be obtained from a reputable visual planning consultant.

Display exhibition

— Will display or exhibition be in special area or will it form part of either entrance/reception space or meeting room?
— What type of material will be displayed, e.g. photographs, literature (leaflets, brochures, etc) or products? What types of units will be most suitable for each of the items, e.g. screens, display stands, shelving or display cabinets?
— How flexible are the systems under consideration? There are various knock-down modular systems on the market, e.g. metal frames with plastic connector pieces and shelves of wood and glass from which a variety of units can be built up.
— How quickly and easily can units be assembled, demounted and moved?
— Is provision made for lighting to be incorporated?
— Do materials and construction appear to be sufficiently robust to withstand wear and tear, movement and storage?

General considerations

— Consider possible hazards, e.g. projecting legs, sharp corners or edges, etc.

— Will the various elements under consideration be compatible with other furniture used and with the overall interior design concept?

— Do moving parts – castors, sliding boards, retractable screens, etc – operate quietly and smoothly?

Finish and maintenance

— Are all surfaces suitable for function and can they be easily cleaned, maintained and, if necessary, replaced? Will they chip or scratch easily?

— Does the method of construction allow for easy cleaning of the floor?

Cost

— Compare the installation, maintenance and in-use costs for the furniture and fittings under consideration.

Table 36 Special furniture and fittings. Levels of specification and manufacturers.		
Basic level of specification	**Suppliers and manufacturers**	
Independent furniture units – tables, chairs, storage cupboards, reception desks, etc – which may be part of matching range.	Alan Cooper	Seating, tables, cupboards, etc
	City Contract	Syba tables and chairs
	Ergonom Distributors	Wilkhahn Programme 840 seating
	Giroflex	Strollgiroflex seating
	Integrated Furniture	Mauser reception and meeting room furniture
	Interspace	Castelli seating and meeting room tables
	Key Industrial Equipment	Seating, tables, cupboards, etc
	Mackmark	Agenda and Deliberation boardroom furniture
	Matthews	Reception and meeting room furniture
	Mines & West	Seating, Embassy conference tables
	Race Furniture	Molecular and Bacchus seating
	Sintacel	Reception seating, cupboards, etc
	Steelcase Strafor	Seating
	Welconstruct	Chairs, tables, etc
	Westnofa	Boardroom and reception seating
Simple, independent display and presentation elements – e.g. pinboards, exhibition screens, wall-mounted writing-boards and projection screens – which may be part of matching range.	Amstad Systems	Display system
	Click systems	Display system
	Gingerbread Enterprises	Instand and Gladhopper 10 display systems
	Magiboard	Range of writing-boards and pinboards
	Marter Haley	Bigscreen, Midscreen and Econoscreen systems
	Matthews	Nobex exhibition unit
	Nobo Visual Aids	Display-It system
	Nimlok	Modular display screens
	OMK Design	Screen system
	SD Systems	Rapid-ex display screens
	Sintacel	Top Track Panels
	Teaching Wall Systems	Functional room dividers, writing-boards, pinboards, etc
	Wilson & Garden	Unique convention writing-boards and pinboards

Medium level of specification		
Coordinated range of reception and/or meeting room furniture.	Antocks Lairn	Reception and meeting room furniture
	Cado Furniture	Cado conference furniture
	Alan Cooper	Calder, Harley and Penniner ranges
	Desking Systems	Reception furniture
	Eglin	Reception and meeting room furniture
	Ergonom Distributors	Master range of conference room furniture
	Hands & Sons	Boardroom furniture
	Hille	Reception and meeting room furniture
	Hitch/Mylius	Reception seating system
	Hopkins Green	System 88 conference room furniture
	Hostess Furniture	Byron unit furniture (reception)
	Lucas	Programme meeting furniture
	Martela	Reception and conference room furniture
	Mines & West	3000 Series conference room furniture
	A. Murray	Reception and conference room furniture
	Office Contracts	Trio Moduli reception furniture
	Plumb Contracts	Fantoni DR conference room furniture
	Race Furniture	Reception and conference room furniture
	Gordon Russell	Conference room furniture
	Scott Howard	System 11 Comforto range
	Steelcase Strafor	Conference room furniture
	Unit 4	Reception and conference room furniture
	Verco	Reception and conference room furniture
Independent display units – shelves, cabinets, etc – which may form part of matching range.	Aluminium Systems	Sheffield Range of instant showcases
	Click Systems	Display cabinets, shelving, etc
	Levine & Son	General display equipment
	Management Services	Mexa showcases and Lit-rak display units
	RT Display	Octanorm display showcases
	Teaching Wall Systems	Range of display units
	Terrapin Reska	Range of merchandising equipment

Wall-mounted writing-boards with fixed back panels and sliding or folding front panels; also with pinboard and projection screen if required.	Sintacel Swedeline Teaching Wall Systems	Top Track Techboards TUA Tuition Cabinet Visu-wall and Meedia 5 total communications environment
	VC Communications Wilson & Garden	Plentybord system Unique range of revolving surface boards

High level of specification

Coordinated range of reception and/or meeting room furniture which forms part of a complete office system.	Alan Cooper	Framac and Contour systems
	Amsico	Reception unit
	City Contract	Aster 22 system
	DP Office Concepts	Five Plus system
	Ergonom Distributors	Modulo 3 reception and conference room furniture
	Matthews	Amseco reception counter
	Martin Neil Designs	Nobo reception unit
	Office & Electronic Machines	Van Blerk Optiforma system
	Vickers Furniture	System E reception unit
	Grant Westfield	KI Cumulus conference room furniture
	Westinghouse	ASD+ system
Coordinated modular range of display components which includes provision for lighting to be incorporated.	Abstracta Construction	Abstracta display system
	Beautiline Tubex	Display system
	Click Systems	Quadrant and Click systems
	Co Design	Insystem
	Gingerbread Enterprises	Clodhopper 1 and System 8
	Latex Systems	Display screen system
	Marler Haley	Multiscreen system
	Olney Brothers	Interplan System 80
	Promotional World	Meroform
	RT Display	Presenta
	Swales-Sofadi	Sofadi display system
	WCB	Triclamp display system
Wall-mounted writing-boards with fixed back panels and sliding or folding front panels; also with pinboard and projection screen if required; plus visual planning system.	Efficienta	Visual planning system
	Key Industrial Equipment	Magnetic wall charts
	Mabco	Telzall board
	Magiboard	Year planner and graph board
	Movitex	Adapta chart system
	Pergola Products	Planpoints
	Sasco	Master Grids and Slotinex systems
	Val-Rex	Teplan system
	Woodcon Products	Trackit system

Industrial and scientific systems, fittings and storage

Independent units and integrated systems for materials handling, production, assembly and storage. (For storage of clothes and personal items, see also p.98.)

Factory systems are becoming increasingly complex and their design depends largely on the specific process involved. Only light production/assembly and manual storage systems are considered here. Manufacturers of electronic equipment and small expensive products (cameras, pharmaceuticals, etc) – for whom change is a fact of life – have found that the relatively new integrated modular factory systems save on floor space requirements and allow layouts to be rearranged very quickly. Before deciding on the appropriate system and level of specification the following must be considered/determined:

Basic requirements

— What network of functions – material storage and handling, component manufacture, assembly, packaging, etc – must be provided for?

— Storage: what must be stored in respect of raw materials, interprocess matter, finished products, tools and equipment? How much of each will need storage and what proportions must be short term, long term or bulk? What speed of access is required?

— What work method will be used – linear assembly; team technology; other? What type of furniture system will be most appropriate – independent elements or coordinated components forming an integrated system? To what degree must workstation furniture be related to and integrated with the storage system?

Flexibility

— What degree of flexibility will be required for both workstations and storage?

— When assessing system/equipment consider how flexibly it can be used (i.e. range of processes it can be used for or range of materials that can be stored), and how easily it can be altered and added to? Will it be easy to obtain additional units at a later date?

Storage

— Determine priorities, e.g. integrated work systems, saving space and/or time, security, etc.

— Consider methods/type of equipment in terms of priorities and material to be stored:

● Shelving: usually metal and adjustable. Various types are available, e.g. slotted angle, boltless, long span, etc.

● Space saving systems: multi-tier (not to be confused with mezzanines: see p.86) – the upper shelves are provided with a floor which is part of the shelving framework; mobile shelving – units move on tracks with manual, electrical or mechanical operation; live racking – gravity flow of goods on inclined roller conveyor tracks.

● Separate independent units usually in a range of separate items which match in terms of design and finish – steel bin units, special cabinets, drawer units, tote box systems, etc.

● Integrated system of coordinated units which may include a range of work surfaces.

— Consider storage of clothes and personal effects:

● What needs to be stored? Are there any special requirements/articles that need to be provided for, e.g. crash helmets, coat hangers, etc?

● If lockers are to be provided, what type (e.g. mesh or solid) and size (full length or 2, 4 or 6 compartment) will be most suitable.

Workstations

— Consider system to be used, e.g. individual, linear or team/group. Which will suit the required pattern of work flow?

— Consider furniture requirements in terms of:

● System to be used – separate units, linked, linked by material handling system (e.g. conveyor).

● Function – assembly, engineering, packing, laboratory.

— Consider special requirements: services integration; local storage provision – low level or high level and fixed or mobile – for tools, materials and personal belongings; space for equipment and machines.

— How easily will layout be able to be rearranged? How easily can workers adjust components of workstations to suit individual requirements?

Construction and finish

How robust is the construction? Will construction and materials used be able to withstand normal wear and tear, and support the weight of persons, equipment and machines?

— Do moving parts operate quietly and smoothly?

— Consider possible hazards: projecting legs, sharp edges and corners, etc

— Are all surface finishes suitable for function – work surfaces non-reflective and able to withstand impacts, heat, humidity, oils, chemicals, etc? Can surfaces be easily cleaned, maintained and, if necessary, replaced? Will they chip or scratch easily?

General considerations

— Security: will lockable stores or units be required for some materials and/or equipment? Are there any materials which must be stored in fireproof enclosures?

— Protection from dust: what material and/or

equipment must be stored behind doors or in drawers?
— Clothes lockers: consider standard type of lock supplied on doors; also, finishes and colours available as standard. Are louvred ventilators or perforated sections needed?

Cost

— Compare the installation, maintenance and in-use costs for the systems under consideration.

Table 37 Industrial and scientific systems, fittings and storage. Levels of specification and manufacturers.

Basic level of specification	Suppliers and manufacturers	
Adjustable shelving – usually steel – of various constructions, e.g. slotted angle, boltless, long span, etc. Of average height (not multi-tier) and with few accessories.	Acrow	Shelving and racking systems
	Barton Handling System	Shelving and racking systems
	Cotswold Storage Systems	Plum shelving
	Dexion	Impex, Spandex and other shelving systems
	Gascoigne Engineering	Keelok 216 shelving system
	James Hill	Long Span and other shelving systems
	Integrated Handling	Shelving and racking systems
	Key Industrial Equipment	Shelving and racking systems
	Link 51	Link Boltless and Handy Angle
	Linvar	Shelving and racking systems
	Remploy	Lundia shelving systems
	Spaceway Design	Minipal and Polypal
	SSI Fix	Shelving and racking systems
	Steel Equipment	Seco shelving and racking systems
	Welconstruct	Spanwel and other shelving and racking systems
Furniture; independent units – workbenches, tool lockers and panels, etc.	Abix	Abix multi-purpose workbench plus range of components
	Key Industrial Equipment	Range of workbenches, cabinets, etc
	Spaceway Design	Range of workbenches, cabinets, etc
	SSI Fix	Range of workbenches, cabinets, etc
	Welconstruct	Welfix and Parade ranges
Clothes lockers – mesh or solid.	Amdega	Pressed steel lockers and changing room equipment
	Arkinstall	Wire mesh lockers and changing room equipment
	W. B. Bawn	Helmsman lockers
	James Hill	Cube lockers
	Langley London	Kemmlit lockers
	Link 51	Lockers
	Michael Saville	Intersan lockers
	Shankey Sheldon	Euroform lockers

	Sheerwood Steel	Lockers
	Sintacel	Locker units
	Speedwell	Locker systems
	SSI Fix	Lockers
	Steel Equipment	Samson lockers
	United Storage	Lockers
	Venesta	Modular locker systems
	Welconstruct	Mesh and solid lockers, and changing room equipment

Medium level of specification

Range of totes, trolleys, units, etc, forming material handling system.	Barton Handling Systems	Storage and handling system
	Cotswold Storage Systems	Plum plastic bin system
	Dexion	Maxi system
	James Hill	Jasil storage system
	Integrated Handling	Storage and handling equipment
	Key Industrial Equipment	Storage and handling equipment
	Linvar	Storage system of plastic tote boxes
	MGK	Storage and handling equipment
	Sommer Allibert	Allibin storage systems
	Spaceway Design	Storage and handling equipment
	SSI Fix	Small parts storage system
	WCB	Mailbox system
	Welconstruct	Storage and handling equipment
Multi-tier storage system.	Dexion	Multi-tier shelving
	Spaceway Design	Panepal
	Welconstruct	Multi-tier shelving

High level of specification

Range of work surfaces, totes, trolleys, units, etc, forming integrated system for materials handling, production/assembly and storage.	Dexion	Maxi, Slotted Angle and other systems in combination
	Herman Miller	Action Factory and Integrated Facility (electronics industry)
	SSI Fix	Handling and storage system
	SMP	Educat – workplace and storage system
Integrated range of laboratory furniture with provision of services, some including a range of furniture for moving supplies.	Cygnet	Range of modular laboratory furniture
	ESA	Laboratory furniture
	Gallenkamp	System M
	Grant Westfield	Lab 800 and Task 500 range of storage furniture
	Gratnell's	Laboratory storage system
	Herman Miller	Co/Struc system
	Matthews	Amseco system
	Miller Williams	Range of modular laboratory furniture
	Morgan & Grundy	Range of modular laboratory furniture

	Nesco	Range of modular laboratory furniture
	Sintacel	Range of modular laboratory furniture
	Vosseler	WLVO System
Mobile shelving and conveyor or carousel storage systems.	Bruynzeel Storage Systems	Mobile shelving
	Dexion	Mobile and conveyor shelving
	FT Engineering	FTE carousel system
	James Hill	Mobile shelving
	Linvar	Mobile shelving
	Remploy	Lundia System F
	Sintacel	Sliding storage
	Welconstruct	Mobile shelving

Solar control: internal

Devices to reduce heat gain in summer through windows and to control glare and daylight. The most effective and simplest way of eliminating or reducing summer heat gain – solar radiation entering through windows – is by using external shading or screening (see p.55). In the case of many existing buildings, however, it is not possible to use this method and internal devices – which are very effective in controlling glare and daylight – may offer a suitable alternative. To decide the appropriate level of specification consider the following:

Basic requirements

— What exactly needs to be controlled – glare, daylight or heat gain?
— In addition to providing solar control, is device required to provide privacy at times? For example, street-front windows or those overlooked from a nearby building.
— What sizes are the glazed areas and what is their orientation? Some form of horizontal screening may be effective on the south side but not on east or west façades, where vertical elements are more functional.
— Is there a special function (e.g. film projection) for which control must be provided?

Methods

— Consider the various methods in terms of priorities after assessment of basic needs:

• Solar control glasses and films. In certain circumstances it may be possible to use either heat absorbing or reflecting glass or, alternatively, a film with the same function which can be applied to existing glazing. These materials are tinted or 'mirrored' and will, therefore, have a pronounced effect on the exterior appearance of the building.
• Curtains: the simplest solution for glare and daylight control, and for providing privacy when required; open weave sheer fabrics may be suitable. Where some heat control is needed, heat reflecting fabrics may be a solution.

• Venetian blinds: various types are available. Blinds placed between the sheets of glass of a double glazed window are not as effective as an exterior device for control of heat, but are more effective than interior blinds. The disadvantages, however, are higher cost and the problems of cleaning and repair.
• Vertical blinds: with tracks top and bottom or top only. Vertical slats on these blinds are normally cord operated and rotate through 180°; also available in tranversing version, i.e. blinds open from centre like a pair of curtains. Generally more expensive than other blinds.
• Roller blinds: spring operated; with a large range of suitable textiles – as well as slatted wood, bamboo and paper – to choose from. Solar control types are also available.
• Pleated sunblinds: usually made from specially treated durable paper and are available either translucent or opaque.
• Blackout blinds: these are available in various types (venetian, roller, etc) and provide maximum light exclusion. Used in darkrooms, laboratories, and for film projection.

Operation and construction

— If curtains are to be used, consider what type of rail will be most suitable. Must the rail be wall or ceiling fixed? What will the weight of curtains be? Must curtains be corded or uncorded? Must rail be concealed?
— What type of operation is required for blinds – cord, crank, electrical?
— Do the blinds and/or rails under consideration operate quietly and smoothly?
— Will the construction and the materials used be able to withstand normal wear and tear?

Appearance, maintenance and cost

— Consider overall appearance effect required and compatibility with interior design.
— Can surfaces and textiles be easily cleaned and maintained?
— Consider durability of materials/textiles as well as fastness of colour to light and moisture.
— Compare the installation, maintenance and in-use costs for the systems being considered.

112

Table 38 Solar control, internal. Levels of specification and manufacturers.

Basic level of specification	Suppliers and manufacturers	
Curtain rails of metal or plastic with internal cording.	505 Manufacturing	Range of curtain rails
	Faber Blinds	Range of curtain tracks
	Gradus	Range of curtain rails
	W. A. Hudson	Rolls range of curtain rails
	Silent Gliss	Range of curtain rails
Pleated paper, or polyester fabric, blinds – translucent or opaque.	Guildford Shades	Accords pleated blinds
	Manor Blinds	Sunway Verosol pleated blinds
	Sampson	Pleatex blinds
Medium level of specification		
Venetian-type blinds for internal use. Slats of stove enamelled aluminium alloy. Control either dual cord or endless cord.	J. Avery & Co	Standard and Unicord ranges
	Bestobell	Sunway range of Venetian blinds
	Deans Blinds	Vistor range
	Faber Blinds	Range of Venetian blinds
	Guildford Shades	Range of Venetian blinds
	MacGrath Bros	Levolar Tiltone louvre blinds
	Norman Hart	Range of Venetian blinds
	Hunter Douglas	Luxaflex range
	Perma Blinds	Range of Venetian blinds
	Sampson	Range of Venetian blinds
	Tidmarsh	Range of Venetian blinds
Roller blinds – spring operated – of textile, wood or bamboo.	J. Avery & Co	Standard range
	Bestobell	Sunway Colourwave range
	Deans Blinds	Vistor range
	Guildford Shades	Range of roller blinds
	Hall & Co	Sunstar range
	Norman Hart	Range of roller blinds
	Hunter Douglas	Luxaflex Rollablinds
	Perma Blinds	Solett range
	Tidmarsh	Range of roller blinds
High level of specification		
Vertical blinds with aluminium tracks and vertical slats of coated cotton, or glass fibre fabrics, etc. Cord operated.	3M	Scotchtint Y2742 vertical louvre shades
	J. Avery & Co	Sundrape
	Bestobell	Sunway range of vertical blinds
	Cosalt	Sundrape range of vertical blinds
	Faber Blinds	Range of vertical louvre blinds
	Guildford Shade	Range of vertical drapes
	Norman Hart	Range of vertical louvre blinds
	Hillaldam Coburn	Solar vertical sliding blinds
	Hunter Douglas	Luxaflex vertical blinds
	Interspace	Telo's 90 sliding curtain panels
	Perma Blinds	Consul range
	Saltree	VCR/2 and, VCR/3 ranges
	Silent Gliss	2600, 2700 and 2750 vertical louvre systems
	Stilsound Blinds	Louvredrape

	Tidmarsh	Range of vertical louvre blinds
	Vertika	Range of vertical louvre blinds
Roller blinds – spring operated – of solar control material.	3M	Scotchtint solar control shades
	Deans Blinds	Solarscreen roller shades
	Stilsound Blinds	Louvredrape Solar V60
Blackout blinds – venetian or roller-type – with matt finish and light excluding channels down sides and across the bottom.	J. Avery & Co	Sun-dark, Slimgroove and Black Shadow
	Bestobell	Sunway Dimout
	Deans Blinds	Durashade
	Hall & Co	X-ray
	Hunter Douglas	Luxaflex Audio Visual
	Norman Hart	Range of blackout blinds
	Perma Blinds	Ridalux and Ridanett
	Technical Blinds	Skyrane 88 and Sunshield 88 non retractable blind
	Tidmarsh	Range of blackout blinds

Signage

System of interrelated signs used to identify, direct and inform.

To be effective, signage should be seen as a system in which each individual element must not only function well on its own, but also be visually integrated with all the other elements and the design of the building and/or immediate environment. It is important to remember that, while signage communicates essential information, it is also an important part of the advertising and identity programme of any company. To help decide on the type of signage and level of specification the following must be considered/determined:

Basic requirements

— Does a corporate image or symbol already exist, or does some form of identification need to be developed?
— Consider what forms of external and internal signage will be required for both visitors and staff, e.g. in parking area, on outside of building, in public lobby, on entrance door, etc. Which, if any, will be provided by the building owner (e.g. directory board in lobby) and which are the responsibility of the tenant?

Categories of signs

— A system of signs may consist of elements from one or more of the following categories:

• Directional: sign indicating direction to be taken, e.g. simply an arrow or a plan-type directory, etc.
• Identifying: sign naming a place or thing, e.g. company name, conference room, etc.
• Informational: sign providing specific information, e.g. business hours.
• Restrictive or prohibitive, e.g. danger, no

smoking, employees only, etc.

Wording and lettering

— List all signs required and determine wording for each; this should be consistent and positively stated with the minimum of words.
— Consider letter types. As there are thousands of letter styles it is helpful to decide which of the four main groups would be appropriate, i.e. serif – identified by short finishing strokes at top and bottom of letters; sans serif – no finishing strokes and characteristically constructed from strokes of equal thickness; transitional – a compromise between the first two types; decorative or display – each design has a unique appearance but these types tend generally to be less legible than those of the other groups.
— What variations are available for types under consideration, e.g. light, medium, bold, condensed, italic and so on?
— Which will be most appropriate in terms of aesthetics; suitability for fabrication technique and material; legibility; compatibility with other signs in immediate vicinity?
— Determine size of lettering and type layout. Should all letters be upper case or lower case only, or capitals for initial letter of each word, etc? What spacing would be best between letters, words and lines?

Other design considerations

— Where are the signs to be located? Consider: regulations and/or restrictions governing position and design; overall effect on building or space; possible obstructions, e.g. planting and other fixed or movable elements; viewing directions, angles and distances; relationship with other signs.
— How should signs be fixed – flush, projecting, suspended, etc? Consider whether

lettering is required on the front and back of some signs and the characteristics of the space(s), e.g. low ceilings or few walls.
— Is flexibility a consideration? Are some signs likely to be changed frequently? Although more expensive, modular signs may answer.
— Consider lighting for all signs. Will ambient lighting provide adequate illumination or will some require spotlights or floodlights? Are any illuminated or neon signs required?

Materials and construction

— Decide what materials, colours and fabrication method to use for both the lettering and the sign background. Choice will be influenced by aesthetic considerations as well as function (e.g. translucent material if illuminated from the back), durability, workability and cost.
— Even the simplest of signs may be manufactured in various ways. The following is a summary of common materials and methods:

● Materials: adhesive film; photographic film or paper; plastic of various types (e.g. acrylics, PVC, butyrates, etc); wood; metal; stone; concrete; neon tubes.

● Methods: individual letters may be cut out (plastic, metal, wood), cast (plastic, metal), vacuum formed or moulded and applied (fussed, glued, etc) to a backing of plastic, wood, metal, stone, etc; letters may be painted, gold-leafed or silk-screened directly on to a variety of backing materials; letters may be integral part of backing, i.e. engraved, etched, carved, sandblasted or cast.

Maintenance and finish

— How easily can signs be cleaned or restored? How permanent is the lettering?
— Are materials well protected against likely damage, weathering, etc? For example, steel must be plated or painted and aluminium should be anodised.
— How vandal-proof are the materials and the construction? Will they scratch easily? Can individual letters be easily removed? How thief-proof is the fixing of the backing?

Cost

— Compare the installation, maintenance and in-use costs for the types under consideration.

Table 39 Signage. Levels of specification and manufacturers.

Basic level of specification	Suppliers and manufacturers	
Sign on access door.	Abbey Craftsmen	Custom-made signs
	Burnham Signs	Vitramel custom-made signs plus other systems
	Clearview	Custom-made signs
	Esselte Dymo	Modular sign system
	Falconcraft	Custom-made signs
	Letraset	Sign system
	Matthews	Murillo nameplates
	Modulex	Sign system
	Olympiad Signs	Custom-made signs
	Olympic Plastics	Custom-made signs
	Edward Pryor	Metalphoto system
	Wood & Wood	Alphatile sign system
Internal signage, i.e. nameplates, doorplates, etc.	Abbey Craftsmen	Range of standard plates in various materials
	Burnham Signs	Custom-made signs of various types
	Clearview	Magnetic modular sign system
	Esselte Dymo	Modular sign system
	Falconcraft	Custom-made signs of various types
	Halo Signs	Range of standard signs
	Key Industrial Equipment	Range of standard plastic safety signs
	Letraset	Sign system
	Malcolm Campbell	Range of standard laminated PVC safety signs
	Matthews Office Furniture	Murillo plastic signs
	Olympiad Signs	Custom-made signs of various types
	Olympic Plastics	Custom-made signs of

	Edward Pryor	various types
		Metalphoto system
	Stocksigns	Range of standard signs – store enamelled aluminium and self-adhesive vinyl
	Tuckers' Sign Division	Range of standard signs
	Visual Planning Consultants	Chartsign
	Wood & Wood	Alphatile sign system

Medium level of specification

As both categories above.	As Basic	
Car park signage.	Abbey Craftsmen	Custom-made signs
	Burnham Signs	Vitramel custom-made signs
	Clearview	Custom-made signs
	Esselte Dymo	Modula sign system
	Falconcraft	Custom-made signs
	Modulex	Sign system
	Olympiad Signs	Custom-made signs
	Olympic Plastics	Custom-made signs
	Edward Pryor	Metalphoto system
	Signs & Components	Custom-made signs
	Wood & Wood	Custom-made signs

High level of specification

Integrated system of signage for access door(s), car park, and interior.	Clearview	Modular system/customer-made signs
	Esselte Dymo	Modular sign system
	Falconcraft	Custom-made signs
	Modulex	Sign system
	Olympiad Signs	Custom-made signs
	Edward Pryor	Metalphoto system
	Signs & Components	Custom-made signs
	Wood & Wood	Custom-made signs
Company signage attached to external wall or fascia (may be illuminated).	Abbey Craftsmen	Custom-made illuminated signs
	Burnham Signs	Custom-made illuminated and non-illuminated signs
	Claudgen	Custom-made illuminated signs
	Clearview	Custom-made illuminated and non-illuminated signs
	Olympiad Signs	Custom-made illuminated and non-illuminated signs
	Olympic	Custom-made illuminated and non-illuminated signs
	Signs & Components	Custom-made illuminated and non-illuminated signs
	Wood & Wood	Custom-made illuminated and non-illuminated signs

APPENDICES

Sources of Information

A. Societies and Institutions

Association of Consulting Engineers, 12 Caxton Street, London SW1H 0QL

Association of Sound & Communication Engineers, 4 Snitterfield Farm, Grays Park Road, Stoke Poges SL2 4HX

British Computer Society, 13 Mansfield Street, London W1M 0BP

British Institute of Interior Design, 22–4 South Street, Ilkeston, Derby DE7 5QE

Chartered Institute of Building Services, Delta House, 22 Balham High Road, London SW12 9BS

Institute of Heating & Ventilating Engineers, 49 Cadogan Square, London SW1X 0JB

Institute of Quantity Surveyors, 98 Gloucester Place, London W1H 4AT

Institute of Materials Handling, St Ives House, St Ives Road, Maidenhead, Berks SL6 1RB

Institute of Plumbing, Scottish Mutual House, North Street, Hornchurch, Essex RM11 1RU

Institute of Solid Wastes Management, 28 Portland Place, London W1N 4DE

Institute of Civil Engineers, 1–7 Great George Street, London SW1P 3AA

Institution of Electrical Engineers, Savoy Place, London WC2R 0BL

Institution of Gas Engineers, 17 Grosvenor Crescent, London SW1X 7ES

Institution of Mechanical Engineers, 1 Birdcage Walk, London SW1H 9JJ

Institution of Structural Engineers, 11 Upper Belgrave Street, London SW1X 8BH

Landscape Institute, 12 Carlton House Terrace, London SW1Y 5AH

National Association of Estate Agents, 11–15 The Parade, Leamingon Spa, War.

Royal Institute of British Architects, 66 Portland Place, London W1N 4AD

Royal Institution of Chartered Surveyors, 12 Great George Street, London SW1

B. Exhibition and Information Centres

UK:

Building Centre, 26 Store Street, London WC1E 7BT

Building Centre, 113–15 Portland Street, Manchester M1 6FB

Building Centre, Colston Avenue, The Centre, Bristol BS1 4T

Building Centre, Grosvenor House, 18–20 Cumberland Place, Southampton SO1 2BD

Building Centre, 15–16 Trumpington Street, Cambridge CB2 1QD

Building Centre of Ireland, 17 Lower Baggot Street, Dublin 2

Building Centre of Scotland, 3 Claremont Terrace, Glasgow G3 7PF

Building & Design Centre, Hope Street, Liverpool L1 9BR

Building Information Centre, Dept of Architecture and Planning Tower Block, New Council Offices, Coventry CV1 5RT

Building Information Centre, Caulden College of Building and Commerce, The Concourse, Stoke Road, Shelton, Stoke-on-Trent ST4 2DG

Building Maintenance Cost Information Service, 85/7 Clarence Street, Kingston-upon-Thames, Surrey KT1 1RB

Building Trades Exhibition, 11 Manchester Square, London W1M 5AB

Design & Building Centre, Mansfield Road, Nottingham NG1 3FE

Design Centre, 28 Haymarket, London SW1Y 4SU

Design Council for Wales, Ground Floor, Pearl Assurance House, Greyfriars Road, Cardiff CF1 3JN

Engineering and Building Centre, 16 Highfield Road, Edgbaston, Birmingham B15 3DU

Northern Counties Building Information Centre, Green Lane, Durham City, DH1 3JY

Scottish Design Centre, 72 St Vincent Street, Glasgow G2 5TN

Europe and Scandinavia:

Bauzentrum Hamburg, Esplanade 6A, 2000 Hamburg 36

Bauzentrum Munchen, Radlkoferstrasse 16, 8000 Munich 70

Bouwcentrum, Weena 700, Postbus 229, Rotterdam 3003

Byggcentrum Goteborg, Masshuset, Orgrytevagen 2, 5–412 51 Gothenburg

Byggecentrum Kobenhavn, Gyldenlovesgade 19, 1600 Copenhagen

As Byggtjeneste, Haakon VII's Gate 2, Postboks 1575, Vika, Oslo

Centre d'Assistance Technique et de Documentation du Bâtiment et des Travaux Publics (CATED), 6 rue la Perouse, 75116 Paris

Centre Rhône–Alpes d'Information et de Documentation du Bâtiment et des Travaux Publics (CXRIDB), Grand Palais de la Foire, Quai Achille–Klignon, 69459 Lyon, Cedex 3

Centro Edile, Via Rivoltana 8, 20090 Segrate, Milano

Centro Informativo de la Construccion, Lauria 117, Barcelona 9

Instituto Nacional para la Calidad en la Edificacion, Plazo del San Juan de la Cruz 1, Madrid 3

Raddenustietosaatio, Lonnrotinkatu 20B, 00120 Helsinki 12

Skansk Byggtjanst, Studentgaten 4, S–211, 38 Malmö

Svensk Byggtjanst, Vastra Vagen 7A, Solna (box 7853, S–10399 Stockholm)

C. General

Agrement Board, PO Box 195, Bucknall's Lane, Garston, Watford

British Gas, 59 Bryanston Street, London W1A 2AZ

British Institute of Cleaning Science, 73/4 Central Buildings, 24 Southwark Street, London SE1 1TY

British Research Establishment, Garston, Watford WD2 7JR

British Standards Institution, 2 Park Street, London W1A 2BS

Building Maintenance Cost Information Service, 85/7 Clarence Street, Kingston-on-Thames, Surrey KT1 1RB

Building Services Research and Information Association, Old Bracknell Lane, Bracknell, Berks RG12 4AH

Council for Small Industries in Rural Areas (CSIRA), Queen's House, Fish Row, Salisbury, Wilts

Department of Industry, Ashdown House, 123 Victoria Road, London SW1E 6RB

Department of Trade, 1 Victoria Street, London W1H 0ET

The Electricity Council, 30 Millbank, London SW1P 4RD

Fire Protection Association, Aldermary House, Queen Street, London EC4N 1TJ

Heat Pump & Air-Conditioning Bureau, 30 Millbank, London SW1P 4RD

Natural Energy Association, 35 Sydenham Road, Guildford, Surrey

Natural Energy Centre, 2 York Street, London W1H 1FA

D. Trade Associations

Association of Building Component Manufacturers, 26 Store Street, London WC1E 7BT

Association of Loading Equipment Manufacturers, 8 St Bride Street, London EC4

Autoclaved Aerate Concrete Products Association, Station Road, Coleshill, Birmingham B46 1HP

Automatic Vending Association of Britain, 50 Eden Street, Kingston-upon-Thames, Surrey

Brick Development Association, Woodside House, Winkfield, Windsor, Berks SL4 2DX

British Blind & Shutter Association, 251 Brompton Road, London SW3

British Carpet Manufacturers Association, Margam House, 26 St James's Square, London SW1Y 4JH

British Ceramic Tile Council, Federation House, Station Road, Stoke-on-Trent ST4 2RU

British Constructional Steelwork Association, 92/6 Vauxhall Bridge Road, London SW1

British Decorators Association, 6 Haywra Street, Harrogate, Yorks HG1 5BL

British Electrical & Allied Manufacturers Association, 8 Leicester Street, London WC2H 1BN

British Flooring Association, 23 Chippenham Mews, London W9 2AN

British Furniture Manufacturers Federated Associations, 30 Harcourt Street, London W1

British Laminated Plastics Fabricators Association, 3–4 Cardale Street, Rowley Regis, Warley, West Midlands B65 0LX

British Lock Manufacturers Association, 91–3 Tettenhall Road, Wolverhampton WV3 9PE

British Plastics Federation, 5 Belgrave Square, London SW1X 8PH

British Security Industry Association, 68 St James's Street, London SW1

British Sign Association, PO Box 4, Beckenham, Kent BR3 3NW

British Woodworking Federation, 82 New Cavendish Street, London W1M 8AD

Business Equipment Trade Association, 109 Kingsway, London WC2B 6PU

Calcium Silicate Brick Association, 11 White Lion House, Town Centre, Hatfield, Herts AL10 0JL

Contract Cleaning and Maintenance Association, 142 Strand, London WC2

Council of British Ceramic Sanitaryware Manufacturers, Federation House, Station Road, Stoke-on-Trent ST4 2RT

Decorative Lighting Association, Moelfre, Anglesey, Gwynedd LL72 8LN

Draughtproofing Advisory Association, PO Box 16, Poole, Dorset

Dry Lining & Partitioning Association, 82 New Cavendish Street, London W1M 8AD

Electrical Contractors Association, ESCA House, 34 Palace Court, London W2 4HY

Engineering Equipment Users Association, 14 Belgrave Square, London SW1X 8PX

Federation of Epoxy Resin Formulators and Applicators, 33 Bedford Row, London WC1R 4JN

Federation of Master Builders, 33 John Street, London WC1N 2BB

Fire Extinguishing Trades Association, 48A Eden Street, Kingston-upon-Thames, Surrey KT1 1EE

Glass and Glazing Federation, 6 Mount Row, London W1Y 6DY

Guild of Architectural Ironmongers, 15 Soho Square, London W1V 5FB

Heating, Ventilating and Air-Conditioning Manufacturers Association, Unit 3, Phoenix House, Phoenix Way, Heston, Middlesex TW5 9ND

Heating and Ventilating Contractors Association, 34 Palace Court, London W2 4JG

Kitchen Furniture Manufacturers Association, Turret House, Station Road, Amersham, Bucks HP7 0AB

Lighting Industry Federation, Swan House, 207 Balham High Road, London SW17 7BQ

Manufacturers Association of Radiators & Convectors, 24 Ormond Road, Richmond, Surrey TW10 6TH

Metal Sink Manufacturers Association, Fleming House, Renfrew Street, Glasgow G3 6TG

National Association of Lift Makers, 8 Leicester Street, London WC2H 7BN

National Association of Plumbing, Heating and Mechanical Services Contractors, 6 Gate Street, London WC2A 3HX

National Association of Shopfitters, NAS House, 411 Limpsfield Road, The Green, Warlingham, Surrey CR3 9RL

National Cavity Insulation Association, 178 Great Portland Street, London W1N 6AQ

National Federation of Painting & Decorating Contractors, 82 New Cavendish Street, London W1M 8AD

National Master Tile Fixers Association, Elvian House, 18–20 St Andrew Street, London EC4 3AE

Partitioning Industry Association, 9 Woodland Close, Hemel Hempstead, Herts HP1 1RQ

Prefabricated Building Manufacturers Association, Westgate House, Chalk Lane, Epsom, Surrey

Society of British Gas Industries, 56 Holly Walk, Leamington Spa, War. CV32 4JE

Solar Trade Association, 26 Store Street, London WC1E 7BT

Suspended Ceiling Association, 14 Green End Road, Boxmoor, Hemel Hempstead, Herts HP1 1QW

Thermal Insulation Contractors Association, 24 Ormond Road, Richmond, Surrey TW10 6TH

Timber Research and Development Association, Stocking Lane, Hughenden Valley, High Wycombe, Bucks HP14 4ND

Wallpaper, Paint & Wallcovering Retailers Association, PO Box 44, Walsall, West Midlands

Index of Manufacturers

Abbey Craftsmen Ltd
Park Walks
Kingsley Bordon
Hants
GU35 9BR
Telephone 042 03 2091

Abbott Bros (Southall) Ltd
Abbess House
39/47 High Street
Middx
UB1 3HE
Telephone 01-574 6961

Ackermann Electrical Systems Ltd
30 Tanners Drive
Blakelands
Milton Keynes
MK14 5BW
Telephone 0908 611780

Acordial (UK) Ltd
Kebbell House
Carpenders Park
Watford
Herts
WD1 5BE
Telephone 01-428 0977

Acrow Storage & Equipment Ltd
Moorhall Road
Harefield
Middx
UB9 6PA
Telephone 089 582 2411

AEG Telefunken (UK) Ltd
217 Bath Road
Slough
SL1 4AW
Telephone 0753 872221

Aerated Concrete Ltd
Northumberland Road
Linford
Stanford-le-Hope
Essex
Telephone 0375 673344

AFA Minerva Ltd
Security House
Grosvener Road
Twickenham
Middx
TW1 4AB
Telephone 01-892 4422

Airflow (Nicoll Ventilators) Ltd
Unit 8
Gore Road Industrial Estate
New Milton
Hants
BH25 6TQ
Telephone 0425 611547

Airflow Developers Ltd
Lancaster Road
High Wycombe
Bucks
HP12 3QP
Telephone 0494 25252

Amdega Ltd
Faverdale
Darlington
Co. Durham
DL3 0PW
Telephone 0325 468522

Amseco Ltd
15 Rathbone Street
London W1
Telephone 01-636 4737

Amtico
PO Box 42
Foleshill Road
Coventry
West Midlands
CV6 5AG
Telephone 0203 88771

Anderson Ceramics Ltd
Dukesway
Team Valley
Gateshead
Tyne and Wear
NE11 0SW
Telephone 0632 874511

Anderson Construction Co Ltd
Cambridge Road
Twickenham
Middx
Telephone 01-892 4444

Anderson GEC Ltd
89 Herkomer Road
Bushey
Herts
Telephone 01-950 1826

Anex Energy Ltd
Unit 18
Belgrave Industrial Estate
Portswood
Southampton
SO2 3AR
Telephone 0703 556866

Anglian Carpet Tiles Ltd
Unit 6
Grange Farm Road
Whitehall Industrial Estate
Colchester
Essex
CO2 8JW
Telephone 0206 46332

Angus Fire Armour Ltd
Thame Park Road
Thame
Oxon
OX9 3RQ
Telephone 084 421 4545

Anmac Ltd
Trent Lane
Nottingham
NG2 4DS
Telephone 0602 582821

Ansamatic Ltd
Viatron House
High Road
London N12
Telephone 01-446 2451

Antifyre Ltd
Vale House
Grove Place
London
W3 6AP
Telephone 01-992 1166

Antock Lairn Ltd
Lancaster Road
Cressex
High Wycombe
Bucks
HP12 3HZ
Telephone 0494 24912

Aquatron (Showers) Ltd
Homer Works
Stirling Road
Shirley
Solihull
West Midlands
B90 4NR
Telephone 021 704 4193/1844

Aram Designs Ltd
3 Kean Street
Covent Garden
London
WC2 4AT
Telephone 01-240 3933

ARC Concrete Ltd
Besselsleigh Road
Abingdon
Oxon
OX1 5LA
Telephone 0865 730025

Architectural Trading Company
219/229 Shaftesbury Avenue
London
WC2H 8AR
Telephone 01-240 8441

Arenson International Ltd
Lincoln House
Colney Street
St Albans
Herts
AL2 2DX
Telephone 09276 7211

ARI Propaflor Ltd
Unit G
Dalroad Industrial Estate
Dallow Road
Luton
Beds
LU1 1SP
Telephone 0582 34161

Arkinstall Bros (Bromsgrove) Ltd
Station Street
Bromsgrove
Worcs
B60 2BU
Telephone 0527 72962/75485

Armitage Shanks Ltd
Armitage
Rugeley
Staffs
WS15 4BT
Telephone 0543 490253

Armstrong World Industries Ltd
Armstrong House
3 Chequer's Square
Uxbridge
Middx
UB8 1NG
Telephone 0895 51122

Artemide
17/19 Neal Street
London WC2
Telephone 01-240 2552

Ascog Lighting Ltd
Nathan Way
Woolwich/Thamesmead
London
SE28 0AZ
Telephone 01-855 0055

Associated Metal Works Ltd
30 St Andrew's Square
Glasgow
G1 5PJ
Telephone 041 552 2004

Avery J & Co Ltd
Sunblind House
82/90 Queensband Road
Holloway
London
N7 7AW
Telephone 01-607 6722

Barber and Coleman Ltd
Marsland Road
Sale
Cheshire
M33 1UL
Telephone 061 973 2277/9-8326

Barkway Electronics Ltd
Melbourn Science Park
Melbourn
Royston
Herts
SG8 6E7
Telephone 0763 62121

Barnes HN Ltd
40 Peterborough Road
London SW6
Telephone 01-736 1391

Barron and Shepheard Ltd
134 King's Street
Hammersmith
London
W6 0QU
Telephone 01-748 0311

Barton Conduits Ltd
Old Birchills
Walsall
West Midlands
WS2 8QE
Telephone 0922 26581/9

Barton Handling & Storage Systems Ltd
Barton Industrial Park
Mount Pleasant
Bilston
West Midlands
WV14 7PO
Telephone 0902 43451/2-43711/2

Bawn WB & Co Ltd
Northern Way
Bury St Edmunds
Suffolk
IP32 6NBH
Telephone 0284 2812

Beachcroft Concrete Partitions Ltd
80 Capworth Street
Leyton
London
E10 8JA
Telephone 01-539 7768

Beautiline Tubex Ltd
Upton Road
Rugby
Warks
CV22 7DL
Telephone 0788 71402

Becker Lifts Ltd
Ealing Road
Alperton
Wembley
Middx
HA0 4PA
Telephone 01-903 8333

Best & Lloyd Ltd
William Street West
Smethwick
Warley
West Midlands
B66 2NX
Telephone 021 558 1191

BICC Pyrotenax
Hedgeley Road
Hebburn
Tyne and Wear
NE31 1XR
Telephone 0632 832244

BICC Vantrunk Ltd
Goodard Road
Astmoor Industrial Estate
Runcorn
Cheshire
Telephone 092 85 64211

Biddle FH Ltd
Newtown Road
Nuneaton
Warks
CV11 4HP
Telephone 0203 384233

Blick International Systems Ltd
Blick House
Techno Trading Estate
Bramble Road
Swindon
Wilts
SN2 6ER
Telephone 0793 692401

BMG Enterprises Ltd
Chapalizod Industrial
Chapalizod
Dublin 20
Telephone 0001 266557

Boulton & Paul (Joinery) Ltd
Riverside Works
Norwich
Norfolk
NR1 1EB
Telephone 0603 660133

Bowater Hills Ltd
PO Box 12
191 Norton Road
Stockton-on-Tees
Cleveland
TS20 2BE
Telephone 0642 607141

Bray Lectroheat
Leicester Place
Leeds
West Yorks
LS2 9BH
Telephone 0532 439793

British Fairwall Ltd
24/28 London Road
Wembley
Middx
HA9 7HD
Telephone 01-903 0332

British Gypsum
Ruddington Hall
Loughborough Road
Ruddington
Notts
NG11 6LX
Telephone 0602 844844

British Telecom
Dial House
151 Shaftesbury Avenue
London WC2
Telephone 01-434 8060

Bruynzeel Storage Systems
Pembroke Road
Stocklake Industrial Estate
Aylesbury
Bucks
HP20 1DG
Telephone 0296 5081

Bullock & Driffill Ltd
High Street
Bottesford
Notts
NG13 0AA
Telephone 0949 42403

Burgess Architectural Products Ltd
Brookfield Road
Hinkley
Leics
LE10 2LN
Telephone 0455 618787

Burmatex PLC
Victoria Mills
Ossett
West Yorks
WF5 0AN
Telephone 0924 276333

Burnham Signs
Kangley Bridge Road
Sydenham
London
SE26 5AL
Telephone 01-659 1525

Burntwood Partitions Ltd
Five Ways House
Hednesford Road
Heath Hayes
Cannock
Staffs
WS12 5EA
Telephone 0543 79912

Bush Nelson Ltd
Stephenson Way
Three Bridges
Crawley
West Sussex
RH10 1TN
Telephone 0293 547361

Business Aids Ltd
3 Whitby Avenue
Park Royal
London
NW10 7SQ
Telephone 01-965 9821/7

BSG Security Systems Ltd
43 Broadwick Street
London W1
Telephone 01-434 2620

C & A Carports Ltd
Bidder Street
London
E16 4ST
Telephone 01-474 0474

C & R Constructions Ltd
Shay Lane
Overden
Halifax
West Yorks
HX3 6SF
Telephone 0422 59311

C & R Lighting Systems Ltd
Anbrooke House
Southfields Road
Dunstable
Beds
Telephone 0582 62423

Cableduct Ltd
30 Selhurst Road
South Norwood
London
SE25 5QF
Telephone 01-683 1126

Cado Furniture (UK) Ltd
The Poplars
South Side
Steeple Aston
Oxon
O85 3RT
Telephone 01-965 9831

Cape Contracts Ltd
Cavendish Court
11/15 Wigmore Street
London
W1H 9LB
Telephone 01-409 1195

Cape Durasteel Ltd
Bradfield Road
Finesdon Road Industrial Estate
Wellingborough
Northants
NN8 4HB
Telephone 0933 71188

Carpets International Contracts
PO Box 24
Mill Street
Kidderminster
Worcs
DY11 6UZ
Telephone 0562 3434

Carson Office Furniture Ltd
36 Croydon Road
Beckenham
Kent
BR3 4BH
Telephone 01-650 4818

Carters
Taco Works
Sycamore Avenue
Burnley
Lancs
BB12 6QR
Telephone 0282 27911

Casaire Ltd
Raebarn House
Northolt Road
Harrow
Middx
HA2 0DY
Telephone 01-423 2323

Cashman Erectors Ltd
Unit 4
Dunmow Industrial Estate
Chelmsford Road
Dunmow
Essex
Telephone 0371 4111

Cass Electronics Ltd
Crabtree Road
Thorpe
Egham
Surrey
TW20 8RN
Telephone 0784 36266

Celcon Ltd
Celcon House
289/293 High Holborn
London
WC1V 7HU
Telephone 01-242 9766

Celotex Ltd
Warwick House
27 St Mary's Road
London
W5 5PR
Telephone 01-579 0811

Cementation Chemicals Ltd
Cementation House
Denham Way
Maple Cross
Rickmansworth
Herts
WD3 2SW
Telephone 0923 776666

Chaffoteaux Ltd
Concord House
Brighton Road
Salfords
Redhill
Surrey
RH1 5DX
Telephone 02934 72744

Channel Lighting
100/102 Norman Road
St Leonards-on-Sea
East Sussex
TN38 0EJ
Telephone 0424 426842

Checkmate Industries Ltd
Bridge House
Bridge Street
Halstead
Essex
CO9 1HT
Telephone 0787 477272

Chieftain Industries PLC
Grange Road
Houstoun Estate
Livingston
West Lothian
EH54 5DD
Telephone 0506 32223/31717

Chloride Standby Systems Ltd
William Street
Southampton
Hants
SO9 1XN
Telephone 0703 30611

Chubb Fire Security Ltd
Pyrene House
Sunbury-on-Thames
Middx
TW16 5BR
Telephone 093 27 85588

Chubb & Sons Lock & Safe Co Ltd
51 Whitfield Street
London
W1P 6AA
Telephone 01-637 2377

CIE Ltd
30 Pembridge Crescent
London
W11 3DS
Telephone 01-229 3224

City Contract Office Furnishing Ltd
Shropshire House
Shropshire Place
Tottenham Court Road
London
WC1 6JU
Telephone 01-631 5303

Cleerburn Ltd
Walworth Industrial Estate
North Way
Andover
Hants
SP10 5AU
Telephone 0264 61331

Click Systems Ltd
Showroom
41 North Hill
London
N7 9DP
Telephone 01-609 4417

Click Systems Ltd
Head Office
40 Blundells Road
Milton Keynes
Bucks
MK13 7HF
Telephone 0908 310737

Clifford Partitioning Co Ltd
Champion House
Birlington Road
New Malden
Surrey
KT3 4NB
Telephone 01-942 6646

Climate Equipment Ltd
Highlands Road
Shirley
Solihull
West Midlands
B90 4NL
Telephone 021 705 7601

Colas Products Ltd
Riverside
Saltrey
Chester
Telephone 0244 674774

Colchester Fan Marketing Co Ltd
Hillbottom Road
Sands Industrial Estate
High Wycombe
Bucks
HP12 4HR
Telephone 0494 28905

Colt International Ltd
New Lane
Havant
Hants
PO9 2LY
Telephone 0705 451111

Combat Engineering Ltd
Oxford Street
Bilston
West Midlands
WV14 7EG
Telephone 0902 44425/44393

Concord Lighting Ltd
Rotaflex House
241 City Road
London
EC1V 1JD
Telephone 01-253 1200

Conder Group Services
Kingsworthy Court
Winchester
Hants
Telephone 0962 882222

Contiwood (Durabella) Ltd
Arisdale Avenue
South Ockendon
Essex
RM15 5TR
Telephone 0708 851441

Alan Cooper Ltd
Burnley Road
Todmorden
Lancs
OL14 7ED
Telephone 070 681 5111

Corewind Ltd
PO Box 5
Carr Lane Industrial Estate
Hoylake
Wirral
Merseyside
L47 4BZ
Telephone 051 632 5448

Cosalt PLC
Fish Dock Road
Grimsby
South Humberside
DN31 3NW
Telephone 0472 58881

Courtney Pope Lighting Ltd
Amhurst Park Works
Tottenham
London
N15 6RD
Telephone 01-800 1270

Crompton Parkinson Ltd
Woodlands House
The Avenue
Cliftonville
Northants
NN1 5BS
Telephone 0604 30201

Crosby Kitchens Ltd
Orgreave Drive
Handsworth
Sheffield
S13 9NS
Telephone 0742 697371

Cube Store Ltd
38 Grosvenor Road
London W4
Telephone 01-994 6016

Cygnet Joinery Ltd
Higher Swan Lane
Bolton
Lancs
BL3 3AH
Telephone 0204 62121

Dahl Brothers Ltd
Scandia Works
Armfield Close
Molesey Avenue
East Molesey
Surrey
KT8 0RY
Telephone 01-941 4153

Dampa (UK) Ltd
Beringsfield
Oxford
OX9 8LZ
Telephone 0865 340471

Dartford Metalcrafts Ltd
Green Street
Green Road
Dartford
Kent
DA1 1JU
Telephone 0322 21151

Deans Blinds
4 Haslemere Industrial Estate
Earlsfield
London
SW18 4SE
Telephone 01-947 8931

Deewall Contract Ltd
Monument Way West
Woking
Surrey
GU21 5ER
Telephone 048 62 64545

Deltaflow Ltd
Showell Road
Wolverhampton
West Midlands
WV10 9LL
Telephone 0902 733221/9

Denco Ltd
PO Box 11
Holmer Road
Hereford
HR4 9SJ
Telephone 0432 277277

Desking Systems Ltd
Tower Estate
Warpsgrove
Chalgrove
Oxon
OX9 7TH
Telephone 0865 891444

Dexion Ltd
Maylands Avenue
Hemel Hempstead
Herts
HP2 7EW
Telephone 0442 42261

Dictaphone Co Ltd
Alperton House
Bridgewater Road
Wembley
London
Telephone 01-903 1477

Dimplex Heating Ltd
Millbrook
Southampton
Hants
SO9 2DP
Telephone 0703 777117

DLW (Britain) Ltd
Block 38C
Milton Trading Estate
Milton
Oxfordshire
OX14 4SD
Telephone 0235 831296

Don Engineering (South West) Ltd
Wellington Trading Estate
Wellington
Somerset
TA21 8SS
Telephone 082 347 3181

Donn Products (UK) Ltd
1 Swan Road
Southwest Industrial Estate
Peterlee
Co Durham
SR8 2JJ
Telephone 0783 861121

Down & Francis Ltd
Ardath Road
Kings Norton
Birmingham
B38 9PN
Telephone 021 458 6571

DSM Industrial Engineering Ltd
Nottingham Road
Attenborough
Notts
Telephone 0602 255927

Dufaylite Developments Ltd
Cromwell Road
St Neots
Cambs
PE19 1QW
Telephone 0480 215000

Dunford Fire Engineering Ltd
Dunford House
City Road
Newcastle upon Tyne
NE99 1SC
Telephone 0632 26121

Dunlop Semtex Ltd
1 Broad Walk
Knowle
Bristol
BS4 2QZ
Telephone 0272 770761

Duro Paviors Ltd
45 Lawrence Road
Tottenham
London
N15 4ED
Telephone 01-802 8040/8046

Dynamit Nobel (UK) Ltd
Gateway House
302/308 High Street
Slough
Berks
SL1 1HF
Telephone 0753 71851

Eastwood Heating Developments Ltd
Portland Road
Shirebrook
Mansfield
Notts
NG20 8TY
Telephone 0623 748484

Ealing Welding & Engineering Co Ltd
Belvue Road
Northolt
Middx
UB5 5QN
Telephone 01-845 5448/
01-841 6314

Edison Halo Ltd
Eskdale Road
Uxbridge Industrial Estate
Uxbridge
Middx
UB8 2R2
Telephone 0895 56561

EGA Ltd
St Asaph
Clwyd
LL17 0ER
Telephone 0745 582 431

Eglin Furniture Ltd
Victoria Road
Sowerby Bridge
West Yorks
HX6 3AF
Telephone 0422 831731

Ekco
473 Foleshill Road
Coventry
CV6 5AE
Telephone 0203 88771

Electrolux Commercial Equipment Ltd
PO Box 18
Oakley Road
Luton
Beds
LU4 9QQ
Telephone 0582 573255

Electronic Alarms Ltd
Belvue House
Belvue Road
Northolt
Middx
UB5 5HP
Telephone 01-841 6251

Elgood EJ Ltd
Industrial Flooring Division
Insulcrete Works
Yeoman Street
London
SE8 5DU
Telephone 01-237 1144

Elite Manufacturing Co Ltd
Elite Works
Station Road
Manningtree
Essex
CO11 1DZ
Telephone 020639 2171 3252

Elliott-Medway Construction Ltd
Glebe Works
Glebe St
Peterborough
Cambs
PE2 8EE
Telephone 0733 52151

ELS (Electronic Locking Systems) Ltd
5/8 Angel House
Pentonville Road
London
N1 9HJ
Telephone 01-278 2161/3

Eltron (London) Ltd
Eltron House
20/28 Whitehorse Road
Croydon
Surrey
CR9 2NA
Telephone 01-689 4341

Enviro-Aesthetic Engineering Co Ltd
9 Albion Place
Maidstone
Kent
ME14 5DY
Telephone 0622 50157

Environaire UK Ltd
Canal Wharf
Chichester
West Sussex
PO19 2PT
Telephone 0243 784178

Erco Lighting Ltd
38 Dover Street
London
W1X 3RB
Telephone 01-408 0320

Ergonom Ltd
38 Warren Street
London
W1P 6JN
Telephone 01-387 8001/5

ESA Furniture Ltd
Esavian Works
Stevenage
Herts
SG1 2NX
Telephone 0438 31355

ESA International Ltd
Esavian Works
Fairview Road
Stevenage
Herts
SG1 2HX
Telephone 0438 313355

Esselte Dymo Ltd
Spur Road
Feltham
Middx
TW14 0SL
Telephone 01-890 1388

Eswa Ltd
32 Monkton Street
London
SE11 4TX
Telephone 01-735 0043

Evans Lifts Ltd
Prospect Works
Abbey Lane
Leicester
LE4 5QX
Telephone 0533 662464

Expandex Ltd
Hitchin Street
Biggleswade
Beds
SG18 8BS
Telephone 0767 312700

Faber Blinds (Great Britain) Ltd
Viking House
Kangley Bridge Road
Sydenham
London
SE26 5AQ
Telephone 01-659 2126

Facit
Maidstone Road
Rochester
Kent
Telephone 0634 401721

Facit Addo Ltd
Hugin House
18/30 Clerkenwell Road
London
EC1M 5NN
Telephone 01-251 0187

Falconcraft Ltd
89/95 Hainault Road
Romford
Essex
RM5 3AH
Telephone 0708 24621/9

Faram (UK) Ltd
31 Sidcup Bypass
Sidcup
Kent
Telephone 01-302 2535

Ferham Products
PO Box 164
Greasbro Road
Tinsley
Sheffield
S9 1TJ
Telephone 0742 446451

Fibreglass Ltd
Prescot Road
St Helens
Merseyside
WA10 3TR
Telephone 0744 693160

Firmin & Collins Ltd
Elgar House
41 Streatham High Road
London
SW16 1ER
Telephone 01-677 2345

Flairline Ceiling Systems Ltd
Downing Street
Smethwick
Warley
West Midlands
B66 2PA
Telephone 021 558 3222

Flexiform
16 Duncan Terrace
London
N1 8BZ
Telephone 01-278 0671

Flos
Heath Hall
Heath
Wakefield
WF1 5SL
Telephone 0924 366446/7/8

Fluorel Ltd
Riverside Works
Broadmead Road
Woodford Green
Essex
1G8 8PG
Telephone 01-504 9691

Fonadek International Ltd
Albany Road
Harborne
Birmingham
B17 9JS
Telephone 021 427 2267/8

Forbo-Krommenie (UK) Ltd
Leet Court
14 King Street
Watford
Herts
WD1 8BZ
Telephone 0923 52323

Fordham Bathrooms & Kitchens Ltd
Fordham House
Dudley Road
Wolverhampton
West Midlands
WV2 4DS
Telephone 0902 59123

Forma (Mann Victor R & Co Ltd)
Unit 3
Mitcham Industrial Estate
85 Streatham Road
Mitcham
Surrey
CR4 2AP
Telephone 01-640 6811

Formwood Ltd
Coleford
Glos
GL16 8PR
Telephone 0594 33305

Fosroc Construction Chemicals Div Ltd
Vimy Road
Leighton Buzzard
Beds
LU7 7EW
Telephone 0525 375646

Freudenberg Carl and Co (UK) Ltd
Lutterworth
Leics
LE17 4DU
Telephone 045 55 3081

Fritztile (UK) Ltd
110 Ashley Down Road
Bristol
BS7 9JR
Telephone 0272 45079

Gainsborough Electrical Ltd
Shefford Road
Aston
Birmingham
West Midlands
B6 4PL
Telephone 021 359 5631

Gallenkamp A & Co Ltd
Belton Road West
Loughborough
LE11 0TR
Telephone 0509 237371

Garbutt GR and Sons Ltd
Longbeck Trading Estate
Marske-by-Sea
Redcar
Cleveland
TS11 6HB
Telephone 0642 485367/483045

Gardom & Lock Ltd
Portland Street
Aston
Birmingham
B6 5SD
Telephone 021 327 4211

Gaskell & Co (Bacup) Ltd
Lee Mill
Bacup
Lancs
OL13 0DJ
Telephone 0706 874381

GEC Claudgen Ltd
South Way
Wembley Stadium Industrial Estate
Wembley
Middx
HA9 0DF
Telephone 01-902 3682/7

GEC Xpelair Ltd
PO Box 220
Deykin Avenue
Witton
Birmingham
B6 7JH
Telephone 021 327 1984

Gent Ltd
26/28 Eden Grove
Holloway
London
N7 8EF
Telephone 01-607 5475

Gerland Ltd
90 Crawford Street
London
W1H 2AP
Telephone 01-723 6601

Gilflex-Key
Tolpits Lane
Watford
Herts
WD1 8XT
Telephone 0923 720177

Gingerbread Enterprises Ltd
19 Heathmans Road
London
SW6 4TJ
Telephone 01-736 6527

Giroflex Ltd
Giltspur House
6 Giltspur Street
London
EC1A 9DE
Telephone 01-236 0653

Glasdon Ltd
Preston New Road
Blackpool
FY4 4UL
Telephone 0253 696838

Goldschmidt TH Ltd
Initial House
150 Field End Road
Eastcote
Middx
HA5 1SA
Telephone 01-868 1331

Russell Gordon Ltd
Broadway
Worcs
WR12 7AD
Telephone 0386 853345

Gough and Company (Hanley) Ltd
Clough Street
Hanley
Stoke-on-Trent
Staffs
ST1 4AP
Telephone 0782 24401

Gower Furniture PLC
Holmfield Industrial Estate
Halifax
West Yorks
HX2 9TN
Telephone 0422 246201

Grab Resins (Leicester) Ltd
Clifford Street
Sough Wigston
Leicester
LE8 2SJ
Telephone 0533 787521

Gradus Ltd
Park Green
Macclesfield
Cheshire
SK11 7NE
Telephone 0625 28922

Grangewood Partitions Ltd
49 Broadway Market
London
E8 4PH
Telephone 01-254 1131/2

Grant International
Universal House
The Hyde Industrial Estate
The Hyde
London
NW9 6PZ
Telephone 01-205 5451

Grant Westfield Ltd
Westfield Road
Edinburgh
EH11 2QF
Telephone 031 337 5346/2252

Gratnells Ltd
256 Church Road
London
E10 7JQ
Telephone 01-556 9021

Greenwood Airvac Ventilation Ltd
PO Box 3
Brookside Industrial Estate
Rustington
Littlehampton
West Sussex
BN16 3LH
Telephone 090 62 71021

Group 4 Total Security Ltd
Farncombe House
Broadway
Worcs
WR12 7LJ
Telephone

GTE Unistrut Ltd
Unistrut House
Edison Road
Elms Industrial Estate
Bedford
MK41 0HU
Telephone 0234 211331

Guildford Shades
Keens Lane
Guildford
Surrey
GU3 3JS
Telephone 0483 232394

Haden Fire Protection
141 Euston Road
London
NW1 2AY
Telephone 01-387 4377

Hall G & Co Ltd
St Georges Square
Portsmouth
Hants
PO1 3AT
Telephone 0705 750212

Halo Signs Ltd
New England House
New England Street
Brighton
East Sussex
BN1 4HN
Telephone 0273 601334

Halstead James Flooring
Radcliffe New Road
Whitefield
Manchester
M25 7NR
Telephone 061 766 3781

Hands & Sons
Dashwood Avenue
High Wycombe
Bucks
HP12 3DX
Telephone 0494 24222

Hanovia Ltd
145 Farnham Road
Slough
Berks
SL1 4XB
Telephone 0753 31351

HAOS Co Ltd
32 Letchworth Drive
Bromley
Kent
BR2 9BE
Telephone 01-290 0245/01-460 2136

Hardall International Ltd
34 Clark Road
Mount Farm
Milton Keynes
Bucks
MK1 1LG
Telephone 0908 648011

Hart Norman (Newcastle) Ltd
Industrial Door Division
10 Redburn Road
Westhope Industrial Estate
Newcastle upon Tyne
NE15 1PJ
Telephone 0632 860256

Harton Heating Appliances Ltd
Eastern House
Hailey Road
Thamesmead Eastern Industrial
Estate
Erith
Kent
Telephone 01-310 0421

Harvey G A Office Furniture Ltd
17/19 Redcross Way
London
SE1 1TB
Telephone 01-407 5964/01-403 4984

Hatmet Contracts Ltd
24 Edison Road
London
N8 8AE
Telephone 01-348 9262

Hauserman Ltd
Hamilton House
3 North Street
Carshalton
Surrey
SM5 2HW
Telephone 01-773 2121

HCP Ltd
Castleham Road
St Leonards-on-Sea
East Sussex
TN38 9NU
Telephone 0424 52755

Heal Products Group
196 Tottenham Court Road
London
W1A 1BJ
Telephone 01-580 3781

Heatrae-Sadia Heating Ltd
Hurricane Way
Norwich Airport
Norwich
Norfolk
NR6 6EA
Telephone 0603 44144

Heckmondwike Carpets Ltd
PO Box 7
Croft Mills
Heckmondwike
West Yorks
Telephone 0924 406161

Henderson PC Ltd
Romford
Essex
RM3 8UL
Telephone 040 23 45555

Heuga (UK) Ltd
Heuga House
1 Oxford Road
Aylesbury
Bucks
HP19 3EP
Telephone 0296 33244

Hewetson JA & Co Ltd
Marfleet
Hull
North Humberside
HU9 5SG
Telephone 0482 781701

Hillaldam Coburn Ltd
Red Lion Road
Surbiton
Surrey
KT6 7RE
Telephone 01-397 5151

Hille International Ltd
Head Office
132 St Albans Road
Watford
Herts
Telephone 0923 42241

Hill James & Co Ltd
119 Staplehurst Road
Sittingbourne
Kent
ME10 2NG
Telephone 0795 21935

Hinchliffe ED & Sons Ltd
Albion Road
West Bromwich
West Midlands
B70 8BA
Telephone 021 553 5561/7

Hiross Ltd
Totman Crescent
Weir Industrial Estate
Rayleigh
Essex
SS6 7UY
Telephone

Hitch Mylius
Spencer House
Brettenham Road
London N18
Telephone 01-807 9324

Hoffmeister Lighting Ltd
Unit 4
Preston Road
Reading
Berks
RG2 0BE
Telephone 0734 866941

Hollman Oswald Ltd
208 Kent House Road
Beckenham
Kent
BR3 1EN
Telephone 01-788 5888

Hopkins Green & Co Ltd
North Building
Metropolitan Wharf
Wapping Wall
London
E1 9SS
Telephone 01-488 0391

Hostess Furniture Ltd
Vulcan Road
Bilston
West Midlands
WV14 7JR
Telephone 0902 43681

Howick Partitioning Ltd
Holmethorpe Ave
Redhill
Surrey
RH1 2NF
Telephone 0737 71411

Hudson WA Ltd
115/125 Curtain Road
London
EC2A 3QS
Telephone 01-739 3211

Humber Contract Interiors Ltd
43/44 Berners Street
London
W1P 3AA
Telephone 01-636 6644/01-637 5583

Hunter Douglas Ltd
Wellington House
New Zealand Avenue
Walton-on-Thames
Surrey
Telephone 093 22 28822

Hunting Industrial Plastics Ltd
Havant
Hampshire
PO9 1JR
Telephone 0705 486161

Husbands LA Ltd
Shelah Road
Halesowen
West Midlands
B63 3PP
Telephone 021 550 1560

Hygienic Engineering Ltd
Dellon Lane Industrial Estate
Halifax
West Yorks
HX1 4PS
Telephone 0422 44631

IBM United Kingdom Ltd
PO Box 41 (3rd Floor)
North Harbour
Portsmouth
Hants
PO6 3AU
Telephone 0705 321212

Ideal Standard Ltd
PO Box 60
National Avenue
Hull
North Humberside
HU5 4JE
Telephone 0482 46461

IMI Range Ltd
PO Box 1
Stalybridge
Cheshire
SK15 1PQ
Telephone 061 338 3353

IMI Santon Ltd
Somerton Works
Newport
Gwent
NPT 0XU
Telephone 0633 277711

Intek Floors Ltd
Burcott Road
Hereford
HR4 9LW
Telephone 0432 277278

Intercraft Design Ltd
Berkeley Square House
Berkeley Square
London
W1X 5PE
Telephone 01-493 1725

Integrated Furniture Systems Ltd
Office 2000
247/257 Euston Road
London
NW1 2HY
Telephone 01-388 9344

Interlite Linear Controls Ltd
Interlite House
Packet Boat Lane
Cowley Peachey
Uxbridge
Middx
UB8 2JR
Telephone 0895 56331/444555

Internal Partitions Systems
Interplan House
Dunmow Industrial Estate
Chelmsford Road
Dunmow
Essex
Telephone 0371 424116

International Computers Ltd
ICL House
Putney High Street
London SW15
Telephone 01-788 7272

International Paint
Stoneygate Lane
Felling-on-Tyne
Gateshead
Tyne and Wear
NE10 0JY
Telephone 0632 696111

Interscan Communications Systems Ltd
39 Montrose Avenue
Slough
Berks
SL1 6BS
Telephone 0753 70821

Interspace Ltd
22 Rosemount Road
London
NW3 6NE
Telephone 01-794 0333

Interwand (UK) Ltd
Old Station House
London Road
East Grinstead
West Sussex
RH19 1YZ
Telephone 0342 21136/8

Iris Lighting Ltd
105 St Peters Street
St Albans
Herts
AL1 3EQ
Telephone 0727 34141

Isoplan Ltd
Upper Icknield Way
Tring
Herts
HP23 4JX
Telephone 044 282 4111

ITT Industries Ltd
190 Strand
London WC2
Telephone 01-836 8055

Johnson H & R Tiles Ltd
Highgate Tile Works
Tunstall
Stoke-on-Trent
SY6 4JX
Telephone 0782 85611

Johnson & Starley Ltd
Rhosili Road
Brackmills
Northampton
NN4 0LZ
Telephone 0604 62881

JRF Panels Ltd
Cater Estate
Kent House Lane
Beckenham
Kent
Telephone 01-659 0981

Kalmar Kitchen Warehouse
Raleigh Street
Gamble Street Corner
Alfreton Road
Notts
Telephone 0602 703419

Kalmar Lighting (UK) Ltd
19 Dacre Street
London
SW1H 0DJ
Telephone 01-222 0161/1543

Kardex Systems (UK) Ltd
10 Clifton Terrace
London N4
Telephone 01-263 1236/01-272 0242

Kerrison Furnishing Ltd
Unit 12
St John's Estate
Penn
High Wycombe
Bucks
HP10 8HR
Telephone 049 481 6331

Kewlox Furniture Ltd
Driad House
Bideford Avenue
Perivale
Middx
UB6 7QB
Telephone 01-997 5444

Key Industrial Equipment Ltd
Blackmoor Road
Verwood
Wimborne
Dorset
BH21 6AT
Telephone 0202 825311

Kidde The Walter Co Ltd
Belvue Road
Northolt
Middx
UB5 3QW
Telephone 01-845 7711

Killby & Gayford (Joinery) Ltd
44/46 Borough Road
London SE1
Telephone 01-928 2732

Kingdom Marketing Co Ltd
Shapwick Road
Hamworthy
Poole
Dorset
BH15 4AP
Telephone 0202 673578

Kittridge Flooring Ltd
Britannia Road
Brentwood
Essex
CM14 5LD
Telephone 0277 211575

Kleeneze Industrial Ltd
Superseal Division
Hanham
Bristol
Avon
BS15 3DY
Telephone 0272 670861/7

Klockner-Moeller Ltd
PO Box 35
Gatehouse Close
Aylesbury
Bucks
HP19 3DH
Telephone 0296 85121

Knoll International
20 Savile Row
London
W1X 1AE
Telephone 01-437 7833

L & D Installations Ltd
Oxleasow Road
East Moors Moat
Redditch
Worcs
B98 0RE
Telephone 0527 27566

Lamacrest Ltd
Crown Works
Cola Bath Road
Harrogate
HG2 0NR
Telephone 0423 66656

Langley London Ltd
The Tile Centre
161/7 Borough High Street
London
SE1 1HU
Telephone 01-407 4444

LDMS Ltd
Phoenix House
217/219A High Road
South Benfleet
Essex
SS7 5HZ
Telephone 037 45 59681/2

Legrand Electric Ltd
Southfields Road
Dunstable
Beds
Telephone 0582 609261

Leiston Engineering Ltd
Howlett Way
Thetford
Norfolk
IP24 1HZ
Telephone 0842 64176

Lennox Industries Ltd
PO Box 43
Lister Road
Basingstoke
Hants
RG22 4AR
Telephone 0256 61261

Letraset UK Ltd
St George's House
195/203 Waterloo Road
London
SE1 8XJ
Telephone 01-928 7551

Linden Pride (Contracts) Ltd
Willow House
22 Willow Walk
Sutton
Surrey
SM3 9SH
Telephone 01-641 0888

Link 51 Ltd
Link House
Halesfield 6
Telford
Salop
TF7 4LN
Telephone 0952 586811

Linvar Ltd
Barkby Road
Leicester
LE4 7LL
Telephone 0533 769181

Lita Display Ltd
190/196 City House
City Road
London
EC1V 2QR
Telephone 01-251 8844

Liteway Ltd
Unit A
Columb Industrial Estate
St Columb
Cornwall
TR9 6SF
Telephone 0637 880015/6

Littner Hampton Ltd
Hampton House
White Post Lane
London
E9 5EN
Telephone 01-986 9131

Louvres & Ceiling Systems Ltd
Unit 8
Nelson Trading Estate
The Path
Morden Road
London
SW19 3BL
Telephone 01-543 3156

Lucas Furniture Systems
616 Wick Lane
Old Ford
London
E3 2JJ
Telephone 01-980 3232

Lumitron Ltd
Chandos Road
London
NW10 6PA
Telephone 01-965 0211

Mackmark Ltd
33 Martens Close
Bexleyheath
Kent
HA7 6AD
Telephone 0322 524503

Magiboards Ltd
42 Wates Way
Willow Lane
Industrial Estate
Mitcham
Surrey
CR4 4TA
Telephone 01-640 9311

Magnet & Southerns
Royd Ings Avenue
Keighly
West Yorks
BD21 4BY
Telephone 0535 661133

Main Gas Appliances
Angel Road
Edmonton
London
N18 3HL
Telephone 01-807 3030

Mallinson-Denny (Bushboard) Ltd
Friedon Road Industrial Estate
Wellingborough
Northants
NN8 4SA
Telephone 0933 224983

Manton Insulations Ltd
Little End Road
Eaton Socon
St Neots
Cambs
PE19 9JH
Telephone 0480 214300

505 Manufacturing Co Ltd
PO Box 233
Bradford Street
Birmingham
B12 0PE
Telephone 021 773 8231

Marler Haley Exposystems Ltd
Exposystems House
Queen's Road
Barnet
Herts
EN5 4DW
Telephone 01-441 1441

Marley Buildings Ltd
Peasmarsh
Guildford
Surrey
GU3 1LS
Telephone 0483 69922

Marley Floors Ltd
Lenham
Maidstone
Kent
ME17 2DE
Telephone 0622 858877

Marlin Lighting Ltd
Hanworth Trading Estate
Hampton Road West
Feltham
Middx
TW13 6DR
Telephone 01-894 5522

Martela Contract Interiors Ltd
210 High Holborn
London
WC1V BP
Telephone 01-405 3938/9/01-831 8771

Martingale Technical Services Ltd
18/20 St John's Road
Penn
Bucks
HP10 8HP
Telephone 049 481 3843-5158/9-5150

Mason Nordia Ltd
Nordia House
Seacroft Industrial Estate
Coal Road
Leeds
West Yorks
LS14 2AW
Telephone 0532 734721

Mather & Platt Alarms Ltd
Titan House
184/192 Bermondsey Street
London
SE1 3UG
Telephone 01-407 9741

Matthews Office Furniture Ltd
PO Box 81
61/63 Dale Street
Liverpool
L69 2DN
Telephone 051 236 9851

May William (Ashton) Ltd
Cavendish Street
Ashton-under-Lyne
Lancs
OL6 7BR
Telephone 061 330 3838/4879

Merchant Trading Co Ltd
Adrienne Avenue
Southall
Middx
UB1 2OP
Telephone 01-575 3388

Merryweather & Sons Ltd
Belliver Industrial Estate
Roborough
Plymouth
Devon
PL6 7BW
Telephone 0752 701212

Metair Ltd
Bridport Road
Edmonton
London
N18 1SL
Telephone 01-803 3366

Midland Veneers Ltd
Hayseech Road
Halesowen
West Midlands
B63 3PE
Telephone 021 550 6441

Miller Herman Ltd
149 Tottenham Court Road
London
W1P 0JA
Telephone 01-388 7331

Miller Williams & Co Ltd
Rosemary Street
Shepperton Road
London
N1 3DU
Telephone 01-226 4856

Mines & West of Downley Ltd
Downley
High Wycombe
Bucks
HP13 5TX
Telephone 0494 34411

Mitel Telecom Ltd
Severnbridge Industrial Estate
Portskewett
Newport
Gwent
NP6 4YR
Telephone 0291 423355

MK Electric Ltd
Shrubbery Road
Edmonton
London
N9 0PB
Telephone 01-803 3355

Modulex Systems Ltd
10 North Portway Close
Round Spinney
Northampton
NN3 4RQ
Telephone 0604 494222

Moore Gieo A & Co Ltd
Throp Arch Trading Estate
Wetherby
West Yorks
LS23 7DD
Telephone 0937 842394

Moorlite Electrical Ltd
Birlington Street
Ashton-under-Lyne
Lancs
OL7 0AX
Telephone 061 330 6811

Morgan & Grundy Ltd
High Street
Cowley
Uxbridge
Middx
UB8 2DY
Telephone 0895 38551

Moveable Drywall Construction Ltd
Arthur Street
Redditch
Worcs
B98 8JY
Telephone 0527 21136

Murray A (London) Ltd
92/93 St Martin's Lane
London
WC2N 4AP
Telephone 01-836 6161

Myson Copperad Ltd
Old Wolverton
Milton Keynes
Bucks
MK12 5PT
Telephone 0908 312641

Myson Domestic Products Ltd
Industrial Estate
Ongar
Essex
CM5 9RE
Telephone 0277 362222

Myson Group PLC
Ongar
Essex
CM5 9RE
Telephone 0277 362222

Nairn Floors Ltd
PO Box 1
Kirkcaldy
Fife
KY1 2SB
Telephone 0592 261111

Neil Martin Designs (Products) Ltd
15 Dock Street
London E1
Telephone 01-481 3034

Neilson & Barclay Ltd
Winton Works
Millerston Industrial Estate
Paisley
Renfrewshire
PA1 2XR
Telephone 041 889 5969

Nimlok Ltd
19A Floral Street
London
WC2 E9DS
Telephone 01-379 7289

NKR Systems Office Furniture
73 Welbeck Street
London
W1M 7HA
Telephone 01-486 7051

Norwood Partitions Ltd
Norwood House
Riverway
Harlow
Essex
Telephone 0279 26741

Nuclifire Ltd
Clifford Way
Binley Industrial Estate
Coventry
West Midlands
CU3 2RQ
Telephone 0203 440011

Nu-Swift International Ltd
Elland
West Yorks
HX5 9DS
Telephone 0422 72852/76811

Oakland Elevators Ltd
Mandervell Road
Oadby
Leicester
LE2 5LL
Telephone 0533 713246

Odoni Ltd
Porters Wood
St Albans
Herts
AL3 6NL
Telephone 0727 50854

Office Contracts Ltd
Vestry Estate
Otford Road
Sevenoaks
Kent
TN14 4EL
Telephone 0732 457636

Office & Storage Techniques Ltd
Harmony Works
Edinburgh Way
Harlow
Essex
CM20 2JA
Telephone 0279 416031

Ofrex Ltd
Ofrex House
Stephen Street
London
W1A 1EA
Telephone 01-636 3686

Ofshred Ltd
Firth Street
Huddersfield
West Yorks
HD1 3AH
Telephone 0484 34214

OMK Design Ltd
16/17 Lower Square
Isleworth
Middx
TW7 6BW
Telephone 01-560 6443/7

Open Plan
The Fairway
Harlow
Essex
CM18 6NJ
Telephone 0279 418211

Opus 4 Ltd
Sheffield Hall
Draper Street
Southborough
Tunbridge Wells
Kent
TN14 0PG
Telephone 0892 22084/32225

Orgatech Ltd
42 Gorst Road
Park Royal
London
NW10 6LD
Telephone 01-965 5611

Osram (GEC) Ltd
PO Box 17
East Lane
Wembley
Middx
HA9 7PG
Telephone

Ozonair Engineering Co Ltd
Quarry Wood Industrial Estate
London Road
Aylesford
Maidstone
Kent
ME20 7NB
Telephone 0266 77861

Parkinson Cowan Appliances Ltd
Angel Road
Edmonton
London
N18 3HL
Telephone 01-807 3030

Panasonic UK Ltd
300/318 Bath Road
Slough
Berks
SL1 6JB
Telephone 0753 34522

Paxwood Ltd
Arrow Road
Redditch
Worcs
B98 8NT
Telephone 0527 65703/60332

Pergola Products Ltd
Leigh Court
Leigh Street
High Wycombe
Bucks
HP11 2QU
Telephone 0494 449145

Perma Blinds Ltd
Prospect Row
Dudley
West Midlands
DY2 8SE
Telephone 0384 214231

Philips Lighting Ltd
PO Box 298
City House 420/430
London Road
Croydon
Surrey
CR9 3QR
Telephone 01-689 2166

Philips Small Appliances
Drury Lane
Hastings
East Sussex
TN34 1XN
Telephone 0424 429141

Phoenix Burners Ltd
8 Prince George's Road
London
SW19 2PX
Telephone 01-648 0964

Phoenix Interiors Ltd
Phoenix House
Sunningdale Road
Cheam
Surrey
SM1 2LS
Telephone 01-641 7444

Pilkingtons Tiles Ltd
PO Box 4
Clifton Junction
Manchester
M27 2LP
Telephone 061 794 2024

Planned Equipment Ltd
Belvue House
Belvue Road
Northolt
Middx
UB5 5HP
Telephone 01-841 6251

Plasmor Ltd
PO Box 44
Womersley Road
Knottingley
West Yorks
WF11 0DN
Telephone 0977 83221

Plastics Marketing Co Ltd
Pounsley Road
Dunton Green
Sevenoaks
Kent
Telephone 0732 460322

Platt Daniel & Sons Ltd
Brownhill Tileries
Tunstall
Stoke-on-Trent
Staffs
ST6 4NY
Telephone 0782 86187

Plessey Communications Systems Ltd
9 Dallington Street
London EC1
Telephone 01-251 6251

Plumb Contracts Ltd
Interiors House
Doyle Drive
Coventry
CV6 6LJ
Telephone 0203 664499

Plunkett William Furniture Ltd
Giltspur House
6 Giltspur Street
London
EC1A 9DE
Telephone 01-236 0653

Poggenpohl UK Ltd
Thames House
63 Kingston Road
New Malden
Surrey
KT3 3PB
Telephone 01-949 5716

Portable Factory Equipment Ltd
Summit Works
Smith Street
Kockley
Birmingham
B19 3EW
Telephone 021 554 7241/3

Portasilo Ltd
New Lane
Huntingdon
York
YO3 9PR
Telephone 0904 24872/21951

Powerlifts Ltd
Caxton Way
Holywell Industrial Estate
Watford
Herts
WD1 8TJ
Telephone 0923 27724

Powrmatic Ltd
Winterhay Lane
Ilminster
Somerset
TA19 9PQ
Telephone 046 05 3535

Powys Industrial Buildings Ltd
Pentre
Nescliffe
Shrewsbury
Shropshire
SY4 1BP
Telephone 0743 81495/7

Precision Metal Forming Ltd
Swindon Road
Cheltenham
Glos
GL51 9LS
Telephone 0242 27511

Presco Buildings
Mochdre Estate
Newtown
Powys
SY16 4LD
Telephone 0686 28520

Prodorite Ltd
Eagle Works
Weanesbury
West Midlands
WS10 7LT
Telephone 021 556 1821

Project Office Furniture Ltd
Manor Road
Haverhill
Suffolk
CB9 8QT
Telephone 0440 705411

Prometheus Appliances Ltd
Wildmere Road
Banbury
Oxon
Telephone 0423 504018

Promotional World (Modular Systems) Ltd
6 Peverel Drive
Granby Estate
Bletchley
Bucks
MK1 1NL
Telephone 0908 644444

Pye Telecommunications Ltd
9 Priestley Way
Eldonwall Trading Estate
Edgware Road
London
NW2 1YA
Telephone 01-452 6411

Pye Telecommunications Ltd
St Andrew's Road
Cambridge
CB4 1DW
Telephone 0223 61222

Pryor Edward & Son Ltd
Egerton Street
Sheffield
S1 4JX
Telephone 0742 739044

Qualitair (Air Conditioning) Ltd
Castle Road
Eurolink
Sittingbourne
Kent
ME10 3RH
Telephone 0795 75461/3

Quiligotti A & Co Ltd
Newby Road
Harcel Grove
Stockport
Cheshire
SK7 5DR
Telephone 061 483 1451

Race Furniture Ltd
New Road
Sheerness
Kent
ME12 1AX
Telephone 0795 662311

Rada Lighting Ltd
Hollies Way
High Street
Potters Bar
Herts
EN6 5BH
Telephone 0707 43401

Railex Systems Ltd
13 City Road
London EC1
Telephone 01-628 4507

Ramchester Ltd
63 Buckingham Gate
London SW1
Telephone 01-222 0213

Rank Xerox (UK) Ltd
Bridge House
Oxford Road
Uxbridge
Middx
UB8 1HS
Telephone 0895 51133

Rediffusion Business Electronics Ltd
Rediffusion House
214 Red Lion Road
Tolworth
Surbiton
Surrey
KT6 7RP
Telephone 01-397 5133

Redring Electric Ltd
Peterborough
PE2 9JJ
Telephone 0733 313213

Reed Harris Ltd
Riverside House
Carnwath Road
London
SW6 3HS
Telephone 01-736 7511

Reed Medway Waste Handling Systems
Aylesford
Maidstone
Kent
ME20 7PG
Telephone 0622 77855

Reinforced Concrete Construction Co Ltd
Delph Road
Brierley Hill
West Midlands
DY5 2RW
Telephone 0384 71443/78079/78611

Reliance Systems Ltd
Turnells Mill Lane
Wellingborough
Northants
NN8 2RB
Telephone 0933 225000

Remploy Ltd
Lundia Centre
Ashton Road
Oldham
OL8 3JG
Telephone 061 633 2351

Rieber & Son Ltd
California Drive
Castleford
West Yorks
WF10 5QZ
Telephone 0977 512121

RGS Communications
52/62 Raymouth Road
London
SE46 2DF
Telephone 01-231 8497

Robertson HH (UK) Ltd
Cromwell Road
Ellesmere Port
South Wirral
Cheshire
L65 4DS
Telephone 051 355 3622

Ronacrete Ltd
269 Ilford Lane
Ilford
Essex
IG1 2SD
Telephone 01-553 2096

Roof Units Group
Peartree House
Peartree Lane
Dudley
West Midlands
DY2 0QU
Telephone 0384 74062

Rotadex Industries Ltd
Magnoid Works
Albert Road
Bristol
BS2 0YF
Telephone 0272 778046

Rowledge Interiors Trading
Little House
88A West Street
Farnham
Surrey
GU9 8EN
Telephone 0252 725735

RT Display Systems
212 New Kingsford
London
SW6 4NZ
Telephone 01-731 4181

RVP Building Products Ltd
A Comfield Road
Knowsley Industrial Park
Liverpool
L33 7UX
Telephone 051 546 2050

Sale Steelform Partitions Ltd
284 Washway Road
Sale
Cheshire
Telephone 061 973 1076

Saltree NT Ltd
152 High Street
Harborne
Birmingham
B17 9PN
Telephone 021 427 5898/6148

Sampson TF Ltd
Tomo House
Creeting Road
Stowmarket
Suffolk
IP14 5BA
Telephone 0449 613535

Saville Stainless Ltd
PO Box 74
Altrincham
Cheshire
WA14 3RP
Telephone 0565 830156

Scandia Steel Ltd
Berkshire House
Queen's Street
Maidenhead
Berks
SL6 1NF
Telephone 0628 20242/3

Schlegel Engineering
Henlow Industrial Estate
Henlow Camp
Beds
SG16 6DS
Telephone 0462 815500/812812

Schwank Ltd
62 Sunningdale Road
Sutton
Surrey
SM1 2JS
Telephone 01-641 3900

Scott Howard Associates Ltd
Weston Road
Bath
BA1 2XT
Telephone 0225 336700

Searle Manufacturing Co
Newgate Lane
Fareham
Hants
PO14 1AR
Telephone 0329 236151

Sealmaster Ltd
Pampisford
Cambridge
CB2 4HG
Telephone 0223 832851

Sealocrete Products Ltd
Atlantic Works
Oakley Road
Southampton
SO9 4FL
Telephone 0703 777331

Securikey Ltd
PO Box 18
Aldershot
Hants
GU12 6JX
Telephone 0252 311888

Service Partitions Ltd
Service House
London Road
Brandon
Suffolk
IP27 0NB
Telephone 0842 811339

Shannon Datastor
700 Purley Way
Croydon
CR9 4NT
Telephone 01-686 0644

Shipton Communications Ltd
Shipton House
Frogmore Road
Hemel Hempstead
Herts
Telephone 0442 47171

Siemens Ltd
Siemens House
Windmill Road
Sunbury-on-Thames
Middx
TW16 7HS
Telephone 093 27 85691

Silavent Ltd
32 Blyth Road
Hayes
Middx
UB3 1DG
Telephone 01-573 2822

Silent Gliss Ltd
Star Lane
Margate
Kent
CT9 4EF
Telephone 0843 63571

Simon R W Ltd
System Works
Hatchmoor Industrial Estate
Torrington
Devon
EX38 7HP
Telephone 0805 23721/3

Simplex-GE Ltd
PO Box 102
Ash Hall
Stoke-on-Trent
Staffs
ST2 9QD
Telephone 078 130 3003

Simplex Lighting Ltd
Groveland Road
Tipton
West Midlands
DY4 7XB
Telephone 021 557 2828

Sintacel Ltd
43/45 High Road
Bushey Heath
Herts
WD2 1EE
Telephone 01-950 1430/1748

Sissons W & G Ltd
Calver Mill
Calver
Sheffield
S30 1XA
Telephone 0433 30791

Slottseal Ltd
Fleming Road
Earlstrees Industrial Estate
Corby
Northants
NN17 2TY
Telephone

Smith WH (Eziot) Ltd
32 Mansfield Street
Leicester
LE1 3DG
Telephone 0533 22514/5

SMP (Lockwall) Ltd
Ferry Lane
Hythe End
Wraysbury
Staines
Middx
TW19 6HH
Telephone 078 481 2225

Sommer Allibert (UK) Ltd
Berry Hill Industrial Estate
Droitwich
Worcs
Telephone 0905 774221

Sound Attenuators Ltd
Eastgates
Colchester
Essex
CO1 2TW
Telephone 0206 866911

Spectrum Architectural Imports Ltd
122 Drury Lane
London
WC2B 5SU
Telephone 01-836 1104

SSI Fix Equipment Ltd
Kingsclere Road
Basingstoke
Hants
RG21 2UJ
Telephone 0256 26511

Stannah Lifts Ltd
Watt Close
East Portway
Andover
Hants
SO10 3BR
Telephone 0264 64311

Static Systems Group
Heath Mill Road
Wombourne
Wolverhampton
WV5 9AN
Telephone 0902 895551

Steelcase Strafor
International Buildings
71 Kingsway
London
WC2B 6SY
Telephone 01-242 21228

Stiebel Eltron Ltd
25/26 Lyveden Road
Brackmills
Northampton
NN4 0ED
Telephone 0604 66422

Stilsound Blinds Ltd
Mersey Industrial Estate
Heaton Mersey
Stockport
Cheshire
SK4 3EQ
Telephone 061 432 5303

Stocksigns Ltd
Ormside Way
Holmethorpe Industrial Estate
Redhill
Surrey
RH1 2LG
Telephone 0737 64765

Stokvis RS & Sons Ltd
Pool Road
East Molesey
Surrey
KT8 0HN
Telephone 01-941 1212

Storad
Belfield
Rochdale
Lancs
Telephone 0706 38271

Stramit Industries (UK) Ltd
Yaxley
Eye
Suffolk
IP23 8BW
Telephone 037 983 465

Strand Contracts John Ltd
2 Patshull Road
London NW5
Telephone 01-485 8615/267 1424

Swiftplan Ltd
Nidum Works
Neath Abbey
West Glamorgan
SA10 7DS
Telephone 0792 812551

Systems Floors (UK) Ltd
Priory Works
Priory Road
Kenilworth
Warks
CV8 1QX
Telephone 0926 59231

Tann Synchronome Ltd
Becks Mill
Station Road
Westbury Leigh
Wilts
BA13 3JT
Telephone 0373 822491

Tansad Ltd
Lodge Causeway
Fishponds
Bristol
BS16 3JU
Telephone 0272 657386

Tarco (UK) Ltd
Savoy House
West Derby Road
Liverpool
L6 1AD
Telephone 051 260 0488

Tarmac Pellite Ltd
Tarmac Wharf
Teesport
Grangetown
Middlesbrough
Cleveland
TS2 6UG
Telephone 0642 452 691

TBS (South Wales) Ltd
Triumph Works
The Willows
Merthyr Tydfil
Mid Glamorgan
CF48 1YH
Telephone 0685 4041 (5 lines)

Teaching Wall Systems Ltd
Unit 185
Walton Summit Centre
Bamber Bridge
Preston
Lancs
PR5 8AJ
Telephone 0772 37249

Tebrax Ltd
63 Borough High Street
London
SE1 1NG
Telephone 01-407 4367

Technical Blinds Ltd
Old Town Lane
Wooburn Town
High Wycombe
Bucks
Telephone 062 85 24311/25360

Telephone Rentals PLC
TR House
Bletchley
Milton Keynes
Bucks
MK3 5JL
Telephone 0908 71200

Temperature Ltd
Newport Road
Sandown
Isle of Wight
PO36 9PH
Telephone 0983 402221

Templan Interiors Ltd
33 Richard Street
Chatham
Kent
ME4 4AH
Telephone 0634 812886

Templestock Ltd
1 Ravenscourt Park
London W6
Telephone 01-741 0625

Terrapin International Ltd
Bond Avenue
Bletchley
Milton Keynes
Bucks
MK1 1JJ
Telephone 0908 74971

Terrapin Reska Ltd
Bond Avenue
Bletchley
Milton Keynes
MK1 1JJ
Telephone 0908 74971

Thetford International Ltd
Brunel Way
Mundford Road
Thetford
Norfolk
IP24 1HP
Telephone 0842 62861

Thermaflex Ltd
Queensway Industrial Estate
Glenrothes
Fife
KY7 5PZ
Telephone 0592 757313

Thermalite Ltd
Station Road
Coleshill
Birmingham
B46 1HP
Telephone 0675 62081

Thermo Acoustic Products Ltd
Palace Wharf
Rainville Road
Hammersmith
London
W6 9HD
Telephone 01-381 5221

Thorn EMI Heating Ltd
Eastern Avenue
Team Valley
Gateshead
Tyne and Wear
NE11 0PG
Telephone 091 487 2211

Thorn EMI Lighting Ltd
Commercial House
Lawrence Road
London
N15 4EG
Telephone 01-802 3151

**Thorn Ericsson
Telecommunications Ltd**
Viking House
Foundry Lane
West Sussex
RH13 5QF
Telephone 0403 64166

Thorsman & Co (UK) Ltd
Thor House
Yarrow Mill
Chorley
Lancs
PR6 0LP
Telephone 025 72 78111

Thorton Bodies Ltd
Pilot Works
Holyhead Road
Oakengates
Telford
Shropshire
TF2 6BB
Telephone 0952 612648

Thousand and One Lamps Ltd
4 Barneston Road
London
SE6 3BN
Telephone 01-698 7238

Thrislington Engineering Co Ltd
Durham Way South
Aycliffe Industrial Estate
Newton
Aycliffe
Co Durham
DL5 6AX
Telephone 0325 320711

Thrislington Sales Ltd
Prince William Avenue
Sandy Croft
Deeside
Clwyd
CH5 2UZ
Telephone 0244 532677

TI Creda Ltd
Creda Works
PO Box 5
Blythe Bridge
Stoke-on-Trent
ST11 9LJ
Telephone 0782 392281

Tidmarsh & Sons
Transenna Works
1 Laycock Street
London
N1 1SW
Telephone 01-226 2261

Toffolo Jackson & Co Ltd
Burnfield Road
Thornliebank
Glasgow
G46 7TQ
Telephone 041 649 5601

Toshiba (UK) Ltd
Toshiba House
Frimley Road
Camberley
Surrey
GU16 5JJ
Telephone 0276 62222

Total Fire Protection Co Ltd
Vincent House
Vincent Lane
Dorking
Surrey
RH4 3JD
Telephone 0306 886166

Trace Heat Pumps Ltd
Trace House
Eastways Industrial Park
Witham
Essex
CM8 3YJ
Telephone 0376 515511

Transline Group Ltd
Catwick Lane
Brandesburton
North Humberside
YO25 8RW
Telephone 0401 42131/6

Transtel Communications Ltd
Station Road
Langley
Slough
Berks
SL3 8DP
Telephone 0753 44222

Treetex Acoustics Ltd
Victoria House
Vernon Place
London
WC1B 4DF
Telephone 01-242 6755

Trelleborg Ltd
90 Somers Road
Rugby
Warks
CV22 7ED
Telephone 0788 62711

Trend Communications Ltd
Knaves Beech Estate
Laudwater
High Wycombe
Bucks
HP10 9QZ
Telephone 062 85 24977

Tretford Carpets Ltd
Lynn Lane
Shenston
Lichfield
Staffs
WS14 0DU
Telephone 0543 480 577

Tretol Building Products Ltd
Tretol House
Edgware Road
London
NW9 0HT
Telephone 01-205 7070

TRF Pland Ltd
Lower Wartley Ring Road
Leeds
West Yorks
LS12 6AA
Telephone 0532 634184

Trox Brothers Ltd
Caxton Way
Thetford
Norfolk
IP24 3SQ
Telephone 0842 4545

Trubros Lifts Ltd
Units 1 and 2
Belton Road West
Loughborough
Leics
LE11 0TR
Telephone 0509 239317/8

Trusound Manufacturing Ltd
Critall Road Industrial Estate
Witham
Essex
Telephone 0376 514101

Twinlock (UK) Ltd
36 Croydon Road
Elmers End
Beckenham
Kent
BR3 4BH
Telephone 01-650 4818

Twinlock Furniture
36 Croydon Road
Beckenham
Kent
BR3 4BH
Telephone 01-658 3927/8

Twyfords Bathrooms
PO Box 23
Stoke-on-Trent
Staffs
ST4 7AL
Telephone 0782 29531

Unit 4 Contracts
42/43 Great Marlborough Street
London
W1V 2EQ
Telephone 01-434 3991

Unidare Ltd
Unidare Works
Finglas
Dublin 11
Telephone 0001 771801

Unilock-Curtis Steel Ltd
Brookside Works
Mill Road
Radstock
Bath
BA3 5TX
Telephone 0761 32841

Unilock Group Ltd
176/184 Vauxhall Bridge Road
London
SW1V 1DX
Telephone 01-828 4651

Unirax Ltd
92 Conington Road
Lewisham
London
SE13 7LL
Telephone 01-852 6112/4360

3M United Kingdom PLC
3M House
PO Box 1
Bracknell
Berkshire
RG12 1JU
Telephone 0344 26726

**United Storage and Partitioning
Systems Ltd**
Dean House
Dean Street
Birmingham
West Midlands
B5 4SL
Telephone 021 622 6331

**Venesta International
Components Ltd**
West Street
Erith
Kent
DA8 1AA
Telephone 032 24 36900

Vent-Axia Ltd
Flemming Way
Crawley
West Sussex
RH10 2NN
Telephone 0293 26062

Versatile Fittings Ltd
Bicester Road
Aylesbury
Bucks
HP19 3AV
Telephone 0296 83481

Vertika International Ltd
PO Box 66
Macclesfield
Cheshire
SK11 7PR
Telephone 0625 611622

Ves Andover Ltd
10 Crown Way
Walworth Industrial Estate
Andover
Hants
SP10 5AR
Telephone 0264 66325

Vickers Furniture
(Division of Vickers Office Eqpmt)
PO Box 10
Hawley Road
Dartford
Kent
DA1 1NY
Telephone 0322 23477

Victor Lighting
Norham Road
West Chirton
Industrial Estate
North Shields
Tyne and Wear
Telephone 0632 595311

Vista Plan Reference Systems Ltd
5 High March
Daventry
Northants
NN11 4QE
Telephone 0327 704767

Voko (UK) Ltd
South Bank Business Centre
Ponton Road
Vauxhall
London SW8
Telephone 01-627 2727

Vortice Ltd
Rodd Industrial Estate
Govett Avenue
Shepperton
Middx
TW17 8AF
Telephone 0932 247734

Wakefield Storage Handling Ltd
Bleachers Yard
Radford Road
New Basford
Notts
Telephone 0602 703141

Walker Crosweller & Co Ltd
Whaddon Works
Cheltenham
Glos
GL52 5EP
Telephone 0242 516317

Walsall Conduits Ltd
Dial Lane
West Bromwich
West Midlands
Telephone 021 557 1171

Wanson Co Ltd
7 Elstree Way
Borehamwood
Herts
WD6 1SA
Telephone 01-953 7111

Waste Compaction Systems (Kent) Ltd
Branbridges
East Peckham
Tonbridge
Kent
TN12 5HE
Telephone 0622 871274

Watco (Sales) Ltd
Watco House
Portsmouth Road
Guildford
Surrey
GU2 5EG
Telephone 0483 503939

WCB Mailbox Ltd
Bayley Street
Staly Bridge
Cheshire
SK15 1QQ
Telephone 016 3305577

Welconstruct Co Ltd
127 Hagley Road
Edgbaston
Birmingham
B16 8XU
Telephone 021 455 9798

Westinghouse Furniture Systems
12/16 Fitzroy Street
London
W1P 5JA
Telephone 01-631 1528

WHN National Products Ltd
190 Ebury Street
London
SW1 8UP
Telephone 01-730 6141/3

Wilkinsons Furniture Ltd
Monkhill
Pontefract
West Yorks
WF8 2NS
Telephone 0977 791191

Wilson & Garden Ltd
Newtown Street
Kilsyth
Glasgow
G65 0JX
Telephone 0236 823291

Wiltshier Contract Furnishing Ltd
18 Verney Road
London
SE16 3DH
Telephone 01-639 8931

Wood & Wood International Signs Ltd
Exton Street
Waterloo
London
SE1 8UE
Telephone 01-928 0412

Woods of Colchester
Tufnell Way
Colchester
Essex
CO4 5AR
Telephone 0206 44122

Worcester Engineering Co Ltd
Diglis
Worcester
Worcs
WR5 3DG
Telephone 0905 356 224

Wyseplan Ltd
Chaluston
Bedford
MK44 3BH
Telephone 0480 75377

Youngman System Buildings Ltd
Priest End
Thame
Oxon
OX9 2HD
Telephone 084 421 2903

Zettler UK Division
Brember Road
Harrow
Middx
HA2 8AS
Telephone 01-422 0061

Zippel (UK) Herbert Ltd
Croespenmaen Industrial Estate
Crimlin
Gwent
NP1 4AG
Telephone 0495 244 933